Louis Hughes

**Thirty Years a Slave**

From Bondage to Freedom

Louis Hughes

**Thirty Years a Slave**
*From Bondage to Freedom*

ISBN/EAN: 9783744732826

Printed in Europe, USA, Canada, Australia, Japan

Cover: Foto ©ninafisch / pixelio.de

More available books at **www.hansebooks.com**

# THIRTY YEARS A SLAVE.

## From Bondage to Freedom.

THE INSTITUTION OF SLAVERY
 AS SEEN ON THE PLANTATION AND
  IN THE HOME OF THE PLANTER.

AUTOBIOGRAPHY OF LOUIS HUGHES.

MILWAUKEE:
SOUTH SIDE PRINTING COMPANY.
1897.

COPYRIGHT,
1896.

# PREFACE.

The institution of human slavery, as it existed in this country, has long been dead; and, happily for all the sacred interests which it assailed, there is for it no resurrection. It may, therefore, be asked to what purpose is the story which follows, of the experiences of one person under that dead and accursed institution? To such question, if it be asked, it may be answered that the narrator presents his story in compliance with the suggestion of friends, and in the hope that it may add something of accurate information regarding the character and influence of an institution which for two hundred years dominated the country—exercising a potent but baneful influence in the formation of its social, civil and industrial structures, and which finally plunged it into the most stupendous civil war which the world has ever known. As the enlightenment of each generation depends upon the thoughtful study of the history of those that have gone before, everything which tends to fullness and accuracy in that history is of value, even though it be not presented with the adjuncts of literary adornment, or thrilling scenic effects.

# CHAPTER I.

## LIFE ON A COTTON PLANTATION.

BIRTH—SOLD IN A RICHMOND SLAVE PEN.

I was born in Virginia, in 1832, near Charlottesville, in the beautiful valley of the Rivanna river. My father was a white man and my mother a negress, the slave of one John Martin. I was a mere child, probably not more than six years of age, as I remember, when my mother, two brothers and myself were sold to Dr. Louis, a practicing physician in the village of Scottsville. We remained with him about five years, when he died, and, in the settlement of his estate, I was sold to one Washington Fitzpatrick, a merchant of the village. He kept me a short time when he took me to Richmond, by way of canal-boat, expecting to sell me; but as the market was dull, he brought me back and kept me some three months longer, when he told me he had hired me out to work on a canal-boat running to Richmond, and to go to my mother and get my clothes ready to start on the trip. I went to her as directed, and, when she had made ready my bundle, she bade me good-by with tears in her eyes, saying: "My son, be a good boy; be polite to every one, and always behave yourself properly." It was sad to her to part with me, though she did not know that she was never to see me again, for my master had said nothing to her regarding his purpose and she only thought, as I did, that I was hired to work on the canal-boat, and that she should see me occasionally. But alas! We never met again. I can see her form still as when she bade me good-bye. That parting I can never forget. I ran off from her as quickly as I could after her parting words, for I did not want her to see me crying. I went to my master at the store, and he again told me that he had hired me to work on the canal-boat, and to go aboard immediately. Of the boat and the trip and the scenes along the route I remember little—I only thought of my mother and my leaving her.

When we arrived at Richmond, George Pullan, a "nigger-trader," as he was called, came to the boat and began to question me, asking me first if I could remember having had the chickenpox, measles or whooping-cough. I answered, yes. Then he asked me if I did not want to take a little walk with him.

I said, no. "Well," said he, "you have got to go. Your master sent you down here to be sold, and told me to come and get you and take you to the trader's yard, ready to be sold." I saw that to hesitate was useless; so I at once obeyed him and went.

### A SLAVE MARKET.

The trader's establishment consisted of an office, a large show-room and a yard in the rear enclosed with a wall of brick fifteen feet high. The principal men of the establishment were the proprietor and the foreman. When slaves were to be exhibited for sale, the foreman was called to the office by means of a bell, and an order given him to bring into the show-room all the slaves in the establishment. This was the work of but a few minutes, and the women were placed in a row on one side of the room and the men on the other. Persons desirous of purchasing them passed up and down between the lines looking the poor creatures over, and questioning them in about the following manner: "What can you do?" "Are you a good cook? seamstress? dairymaid?"--this to the women, while the men would be questioned as to their line of work: "Can you plow? Are you a blacksmith? Have you ever cared for horses? Can you pick cotton rapidly?" Sometimes the slave would be required to open his mouth that the purchaser might examine the teeth and form some opinion as to his age and physical soundness; and if it was suspected that a slave had been beaten a good deal he would be required to step into another room and undress. If the person desiring to buy found the slave badly scarred by the common usage of whipping, he would say at once to the foreman: "Why! this slave is not worth much, he is all scarred up. No, I don't want him; bring me in another to look at." Slaves without scars from whipping and looking well physically always sold readily. They were never left long in the yard. It was expected that all the slaves in the yard for sale would be neatly dressed and clean before being brought into the show-room. It was the foreman's business to see that each one was presentable.

### SLAVE WHIPPING AS A BUSINESS.

Whipping was done at these markets, or trader's yards, all the time. People who lived in the city of Richmond would send their slaves here for punishment. When any one wanted a slave whipped he would send a note to that effect with the servant to the trader. Any petty offense on the part of a slave was sufficient to subject the offender to this brutal treatment. Owners who affected culture and refinement preferred to send a servant to the yard for punishment to inflicting it themselves. It saved them trouble, they said, and possibly a slight wear and tear of feeling. For this service the owner was charged a certain sum for each slave, and the earnings of the traders from this source formed a very large part of the profits of his business. The yard I was in had a regular whipping post to which they tied the slave, and gave him "nine-and-thirty," as it was called, meaning thirty-nine lashes as hard as they could lay it on. Men were stripped of their shirts in preparation for the whipping, and women had to take off their dresses from the shoulders to the waist. These whippings were not so severe as when the slaves were stripped entirely of their clothes, as was generally the case on the plantations where slaves were owned by the dozen. I saw many cases of whipping while I was in the yard. Sometimes I was so frightened that I trembled violently, for I had never seen anything like it before.

### SOLD IN THE MARKET.

I was only in the yard a short time before I was

bought by one George Reid who lived in Richmond. He had no wife, but an old lady kept house for him and his three sons. At this time he had a place in the postoffice, but soon after I came there he lost it. He then moved into the country upon a farm of about one thousand acres, enclosed by a cedar hedge. The house was a plain frame structure upon a stone basement and contained four rooms. It was surrounded with shrubbery, and was a pleasant country seat. But I did not like it here. I grieved continually about my mother. It came to me, more and more plainly, that I would never see her again. Young and lonely as I was, I could not help crying, oftentimes for hours together. It was hard to get used to being away from my mother. I remember well "Aunt Sylvia," who was the cook in the Reid household. She was very kind to me and always spoke consolingly to me, especially if I had been blue, and had had one of my fits of crying. At these times she would always bake me an ash cake for supper, saying to me: "My child, don't cry; 'Aunt Sylvia' will look after you." This ash cake was made of corn meal and water, a little salt to make it palatable, and was baked by putting it between cabbage leaves and covering it with hot ashes. A sweeter or more delicious cake one could not desire, and it was common upon the tables of all the Virginia farmers. I always considered it a great treat to get one of these cakes from "Aunt Sylvia."

The appellations of "aunt" and "uncle" for the older slaves were not only common among the blacks, but the whites also addressed them in the same way.

### ON THE AUCTION BLOCK

I was sick a great deal—in fact, I had suffered with chills and fever ever since Mr. Reid bought me. He, therefore, concluded to sell me, and, in November, 1844, he took me back to Richmond, placing me in the Exchange building, or auction rooms, for the sale of slaves. The sales were carried on in a large hall where those interested in the business sat around a large block or stand, upon which the slave to be sold was placed, the auctioneer standing beside him. When I was placed upon the block, a Mr. McGee came up and felt of me and asked me what I could do. "You look like a right smart nigger," said he, "Virginia always produces good darkies." Virginia was the mother of slavery, and it was held by many that she had the best slaves. So when Mr. McGee found I was born and bred in that state he seemed satisfied.

The bidding commenced, and I remember well when the auctioneer said: "Three hundred eighty dollars — once, twice and sold to Mr. Edward McGee." He was a rich cotton planter of Pontotoc, Miss. As near as I can recollect, I was not more than twelve years of age, so did not sell for very much.

### PRICE OF SLAVES.

Servant women sold for $500 to $700, and sometimes as high as $800 when possessing extra qualifications. A house maid, bright in looks, strong and well formed, would sell for $1,000 to $1,200. Bright mulatto girls, well versed in sewing and knitting, would sometimes bring as high as $1,800, especially if a Virginian or a Kentuckian. Good blacksmiths sold for $1,600 to $1,800. When the slaves were put upon the block they were always sold to the highest bidder. Mr. McGee, or "Boss," as I soon learned to call him, bought sixty other slaves before he bought me, and they were started in a herd for Atlanta, Ga., on foot.

### STARTED FOR A COTTON PLANTATION.

Boss, myself and ten others met them there. We then started for Pontotoc, Miss. On our way we stopped at Edenton, Ga., where Boss sold twenty-one of the sixty slaves. We then proceeded on our way, Boss by rail and we on foot, or in the wagon. We went about twenty miles a day. I remember, as we passed along, every white man we met was yelling, "Hurrah for Polk and Dallas!" They were feeling good, for election had given them the men that they wanted. The man who had us in charge joined with those we met in the hurrahing. We were afraid to ask them the reason for their yelling, as that would have been regarded as an impertinence, and probably would have caused us all to be whipped.

### MY MISSISSIPPI HOME.

At length, after a long and wearisome journey, we reached Pontotoc, McGee's home, on Christmas eve. Boss took me into the house and into the sitting room, where all the family were assembled, and presented me as a Christmas gift to the madam, his wife.

My boss, as I remember him, was a tall, raw-boned man, but rather distinguished in looks, with a fine carriage, brilliant in intellect, and considered one of the wealthiest and most successful planters of his time. Mrs. McGee was a handsome, stately lady, about thirty years of age, brunette in complexion, faultless in figure and imperious in manner. I think that they were of Scotch descent. There were four children, Emma, Willie, Johnnie and Jimmie. All looked at me, and thought I was "a spry little fellow." I was very shy and did not say much, as everything was strange to me. I was put to sleep that night on a pallet on the floor in the dining room, using an old quilt as a covering. The next morning was Christmas, and it seemed to be a custom to have egg-nóg before breakfast. The process of making this was new and interesting to me. I saw them whip the whites of eggs, on a platter, to a stiff froth; the yolks were thoroughly beaten in a large bowl, sugar and plenty of good brandy were added, and the whites of the eggs and cream were then stirred in, a little nutmeg grated on top of each glass when filled for serving. This was a delicious drink, and the best of all was, there was plenty of it. I served this to all the family, and, as there were also visiting relatives present, many glasses were required, and I found the tray so heavy I could hardly carry it. I helped myself, after the service was finished, and I was delighted, for I had never tasted anything so fine before.

My boss told me I was to wait on the madam, do any errand necessary, attend to the dining room—in fact I was installed as general utility boy. It was different from the quiet manner of life I had seen before coming here—it kept my spirits up for some time. I thought of my mother often, but I was gradually growing to the idea that it was useless to cry, and I tried hard to overcome my feelings.

### PLANTATION LIFE.

As already stated, it was Christmas morning, and, after breakfast, I saw the cook hurrying, and when I went out into the yard, everywhere I looked slaves met my view. I never saw so many slaves at one time before. In Virginia we did not have such large farms. There were no extensive cotton plantations, as in Mississippi. I shall never forget the dinner that day—it was a feast fit for a king, so varied and lavish was the bill of fare. The next attraction for me was the farm hands getting their Christmas rations. Each was given a pint of flour of which they made biscuit, which were called "Billy Seldom," because biscuit were very rare with them. Their daily food was corn bread, which they called "Johnny Constant," as they had it constantly. In addition to the flour each received a piece of bacon or fat meat, from which they got the shortening for their biscuit.

The cracklings from the rendering of lard were also used by the slaves for shortening. The hands were allowed four days off at Christmas, and if they worked on these days, as some of them did, they got fifty cents a day for chopping. It was not common to have chopping done during the holidays; some planters, however, found it convenient thus to get it out of the way for the work which came after Christmas.

### THE GREAT HOUSE.

I soon became familiar with my work in the house and with the neighborhood, as I often had to carry notes for Boss to neighboring farmers, as well as to carry the mail to and from the postoffice. The "great house," as the dwelling of the master was called, was two stories high, built of huge logs, chinked and daubed and whitewashed. It was divided, from front to rear, by a hall twenty-five feet long and twelve feet wide, and on each side of the hall, in each story, was one large room with a large fire-place. There were but four rooms in all, yet these were so large that they were equal to at least six of our modern rooms. The kitchen was not attached to the main building, but was about thirty feet to the rear. This was the common mode of building in the south in those days. The two bedrooms upstairs were very plain in furnishings, but neat and comfortable, judged by the standard of the times. A wing was added to the main building for dining room. In rear of the kitchen was the milk or dairy house, and beyond this the smoke house for curing the meat. In line with these buildings, and still further to the rear, was the overseer's house. Near the milk house was a large tree, and attached to the trunk was a lever; and here was where the churning was done, in which I had always to assist. This establishment will serve as a sample of many of those on the large plantations in the south. The main road from Pontotoc to Holly Springs, one of the great thoroughfares of the state and a stage route, passed near the house, and through the center of the farm. On each side of this road was a fence, and in the corners of both fences, extending for a mile, were planted peach trees, which bore excellent fruit in great profusion.

### HOUSE SERVANT AND ERRAND BOY.

My first work in the morning was to dust the parlor and hall and arrange the dining room. It came awkward to me at first, but, after the madam told me how, I soon learned to do it satisfactorily. Then I had to wait on the table, sweep the large yard every morning with a brush broom and go for the mail once a week. I used to get very tired, for I was young and consequently not strong. Aside from these things which came regularly, I had to help the madam in warping the cloth. I dreaded this work, for I always got my ears boxed if I did not or could not do the work to suit her. She always made the warp herself and put it in, and I had to hand her the thread as she put it through the harness. I would get very tired at this work and, like any child, wanted to be at play, but I could not remember that the madam ever gave me that privilege. Saddling the horse at first was troublesome to me, but Boss was constant in his efforts to teach me, and, after many trials, I learned the task satisfactorily to the master and to bring the horse to the door when he wished to go out for business or pleasure. Riding horseback was common for both ladies and gentlemen, and sometimes I would have to saddle three or more horses when Boss, the madam, a friend or friends desired a ride. Bird hunting parties were common and were greatly enjoyed, by the young people especially. Boss always invited some of the young people of the neighborhood to these parties and they never failed to put in an appearance. Williams, Bradford and Freeman were the sons of rich planters, and were always participants in this sport, and their young lady friends joined in it as on-lookers. The young men singing and whistling to the birds, I in the meantime setting the net. As soon as I had got the net in order they would approach the birds slowly, driving them into it. There was great laughter and excitement if they were successful in catching a fine flock.

## CRUEL TREATMENT.

I was but a lad, yet I can remember well the cruel treatment I received. Some weeks it seemed I was whipped for nothing, just to please my mistress' fancy. Once, when I was sent to town for the mail and had started back, it was so dark and rainy my horse got away from me and I had to stay all night in town. The next morning when I got back home I had a severe whipping, because the master was expecting a letter containing money and was disappointed in not receiving it that night, as he was going to Panola to spend Christmas. However, the day came and all the family went except me. During the time they were gone the overseer whipped a man so terribly with the "bull whip" that I had to go for the doctor, and when Dr. Heningford, the regular family physician, came, he said it was awful—such cruel treatment, and he complained about it. It was common for a slave to get an "over-threshing," that is, to be whipped too much. The poor man was cut up so badly all over that the doctor made a bran poultice and wrapped his entire body in it. This was done to draw out the inflammation. It seems the slave had been sick, and had killed a little pig when he became well enough to go to work, as his appetite craved hearty food, and he needed it to give him strength for his tasks. For this one act, comparatively trivial, he was almost killed. The idea never seemed to occur to the slave holders that these slaves were getting no wages for their work and, therefore, had nothing with which to procure what, at times, was necessary for their health and strength palatable and nourishing food. When the slaves took anything the masters called it stealing, yet they were stealing the slaves' time year after year. When Boss came home he was called on by the town officials, for the case had been reported to them. Boss, however, got out of it by saying that he was not at home when the trouble occurred. The poor slave was sick from his ill treatment some four or five months, and when he recovered there was a running sore left on his body, from the deep cuts of the whip, which never healed. I can not forget how he looked, the sore was a sickening sight; yet, when he was able to walk he had to return to work in the field.

I had not been at Pontotoc very long when I saw the hounds run a slave, by name Ben Lyon. "Old Ben," as he was called, ran away and had been gone a week when he was seen by a woman who " told on him," and then I was sent to get the man who had trained dogs, or hounds as they were called. The dogs ran the slave about ten miles when they lost track at a creek, but he was caught that night in a farmer's house getting something to eat.

### INSTRUCTIONS IN MEDICINE.

After some time, Boss began to tell me the names of medicines and their properties. I liked this and seemed to grasp the idea very well. After giving me a number of names he would make me repeat them. Then he would tell me the properties of each medicine named, how it was used and for what purpose and how much constituted a dose. He would drill me in all this until I knew it and, in a short time, he would add other names to the list. He always showed me each medicine named and had me smell and carefully examine it that I might know it when seen again. I liked this, and used to wish that I was as wise as my master. He was very precise, steady and gentle in any case of sickness, and, although he had long retired from the medical world, all recognized his merit wherever he went. I used to go to the woods and gather slippery elm, alum root and the roots of wild cherry and poplar, for we used all these in compounding medicines for the servants.

THE OVERSEER—WHIPPINGS AND OTHER CRUELTIES.

The overseer was a man hired to look after the farm and whip the slaves. Very often they were not only cruel, but barbarous. Every farmer or planter considered an overseer a necessity. As a rule, there was also on each plantation, a foreman—one of the brighter slaves, who was held responsible for the slaves under him, and whipped if they did not come up to the required task. There was, too, a forewoman, who, in like manner, had charge of the female slaves, and also the boys and girls from twelve to sixteen years of age, and all the old people that were feeble.

This was called the trash gang. Ah! it would make one's heart ache to see those children and how they were worked. Cold, frosty mornings, the little ones would be crying from cold; but they had to keep on. Aunt Polly, our forewoman, was afraid to allow them to run to get warm, for fear the overseer would see them. Then she would be whipped, and he would make her whip all of the gang. At length, I became used to severe treatment of the slaves; but, every little while something would happen to make me wish I were dead. Everything was in a bustle—always there was slashing and whipping. I remember when Boss made a change in our overseer. It was the beginning of the year. Riley, one of the slaves, who was a principal plower, was not on hand for work one Monday morning, having been delayed in fixing the bridle of his mule, which the animal, for lack of something better, perhaps, had been vigorously chewing and rendered nearly useless. He was, therefore, considerably behind time, when he reached the field. Without waiting to learn what was the reason for the delay, the overseer sprang upon him with his bull whip, which was about seven feet long, lashing him with all his strength, every stroke leaving its mark upon the poor man's body, and finally the knot at the end of the whip buried itself in the fleshy part of the arm, and there came around it a festering sore. He suffered greatly with it, until one night his brother took out the knot, when the poor fellow was asleep, for he could not bear any one to touch it when he was awake. It was awful to hear the cracking of that whip as it was laid about Riley—one would have thought that an ox team had gotten into the mire, and was being whipped out, so loud and sharp was the noise!

I usually slept in the dining room on the floor. Early one morning an old slave, by name of "Uncle Jim," came and knocked at the window, and upon my jumping up and going to him, he told me to tell Boss that Uncle Jim was there. He had run away, some time before, and, for some reason, had returned. Boss, upon hearing the news, got up and sent me to tell the overseer to come at once. He came, and, taking the bull whip, a cowhide and a lot of peach-tree switches, he and Boss led Uncle Jim back into the cow lot, on the side of the hill, where they drove four stakes in the ground, and, laying him flat on his face, tied his hands and feet to these stakes. After whipping him,

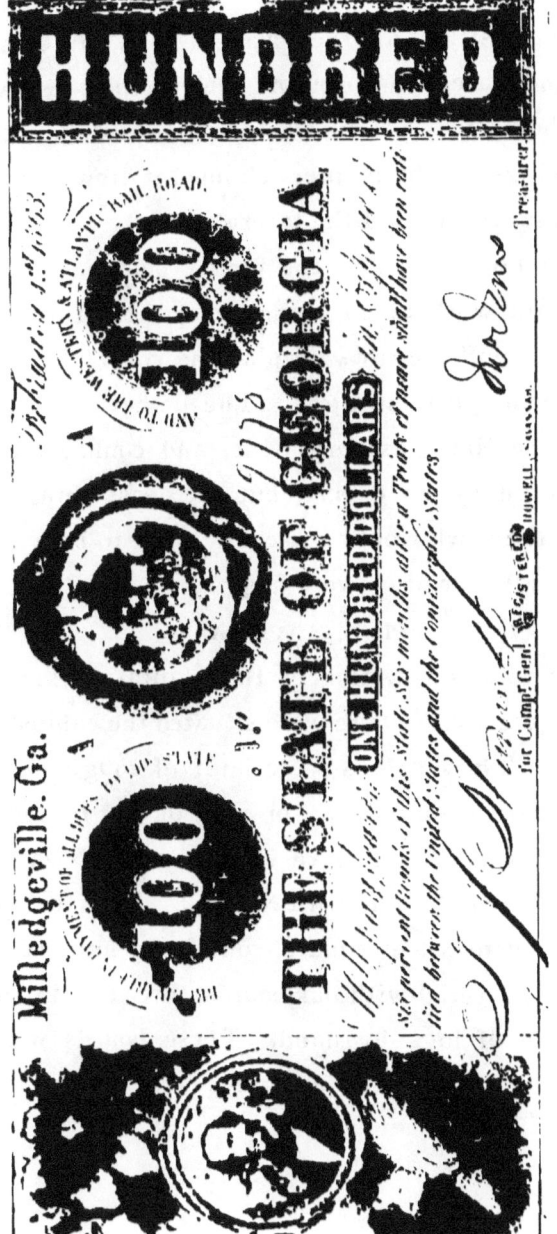

in this position, all they wanted to, a pail of strong salt and water was brought, and the poor fellow was "washed down." This washing was customary, after whippings, as the planters claimed it drew out all the soreness, and healed the lacerated flesh.

Upon one occasion, the family being away, I was left extra work to do, being set to help three fellow slaves lay off the rows for planting corn. We did not get them quite straight. The deviation we made from the line was very little, and could scarcely be seen, even by an expert; but the least thing wrong about the work would cause any slave to be whipped, and so all four of us were flogged.

### THE SLAVE CABIN.

There was a section of the plantation known as "the quarters," where were situated the cabins of the slaves. These cabins were built of rough logs, and daubed with the red clay or mud of the region. No attempt was made to give them a neat appearance—they were not even whitewashed. Each cabin was about fourteen feet square, containing but one room, and was covered with oak boards, three feet in length, split out of logs by hand. These boards were not nailed on, but held in their places by what were termed weight-poles laid across them at right angles. There were in each room two windows, a door and a large, rude fire-place. The door and window frames, or facings, were held in their places by wooden pins, nails being used only in putting the doors together. The interior of the cabins had nothing more attractive than the outside—there was no plastering and only a dirt floor. The furniture consisted of one bed, a plain board table and some benches made by the slaves themselves. Sometimes a cabin was occupied by two or more families, in which case the number of beds was increased proportionately. For light a grease lamp was used, which was made of iron, bowl shaped, by a blacksmith. The bowl was filled with grease and a rag or wick placed in it, one end resting on the edge for lighting. These lamps gave a good light, and were in general use among the slaves. Tallow candles were a luxury, never seen except in the "great houses" of the planters. The only light for outdoors used by the slaves was a torch made by binding together a bundle of small sticks or splinters.

### COTTON RAISING.

After the selection of the soil most suitable for cotton, the preparation of it was of vital importance.

The land was deeply plowed, long enough before the time for planting to allow the spring rains to settle it. Then it was thrown into beds or ridges by turning furrows both ways toward a given center. The seed was planted at the rate of one hundred pounds per acre. The plant made its appearance in about ten days after planting, if the weather was favorable. Early planting, however, followed by cold, stormy weather frequently caused the seed to rot. As soon as the third leaf appeared the process of scraping commenced, which consisted of cleaning the ridge with hoes of all superflous plants and all weeds and grass. After this a narrow plow known as a "bull tongue," was used to turn the loose earth around the plant and cover up any grass not totally destroyed by the hoes. If the surface was very rough the hoes followed, instead of preceding, the plow to unearth those plants that may have been partially covered. The slaves often acquired great skill in these operations, running plows within two inches of the stalks, and striking down weeds within half an inch with their hoes, rarely touching a leaf of the cotton. Subsequent plowing, alternating with hoeing, usually occurred once in twenty days. There was danger in deep plowing of injuring the roots, and this was avoided, except in the middle of rows in wet seasons when it was necessary to bury and more effectually kill the grass. The implements used in the culture of cotton were shovels, hoes, sweeps, cultivators, harrows and two kinds of plows. It required four months, under the most favorable circumstances, for cotton to attain its full growth. It was usually planted about the 1st of April, or from March 20th to April 10th, bloomed about the 1st of June and the first balls opened about August 15th, when picking commenced. The blooms come out in the morning and are fully developed by noon, when they are a pure white. Soon after meridian they begin to exhibit reddish streaks, and next morning are a clear pink. They fall off by noon of the second day.

### THE COTTON WORM.

A cut worm was troublesome sometimes; but the plants were watched very carefully, and as soon as any signs of worms were seen work for their destruction was commenced. The majority of the eggs were laid upon the calyx and involucre. The worm, after gnawing through its enclosed shell, makes its first meal upon the part of the plant upon which the egg was laid, be it leaf, stem or involucre. If it were laid upon the leaf, as was usually the case, it might be three days before the worm reached the boll; but were the eggs laid upon the involucre the worm pierced through within twenty-four hours after hatching. The newly hatched boll worm walks like a geometrical larva or looper, a measuring worm as it was called. This is easily explained by the fact that while in the full grown worm the abdominal legs, or pro legs, are nearly equal in length, in the newly hatched worm the second pair are slightly shorter than the third, and the first pair are shorter and slenderer than the second—a state of things approaching that in the full grown cotton worm, though the difference in size in the former case is not nearly so marked as in the latter. This method of walking is lost with the first or second molt. There is nothing remarkable about these young larvæ. They seem to be thicker in proportion to their length than the young cotton worms, and they have not so delicate and transparent an appearance. Their heads are black and their bodies seem already to have begun to vary in color. The body above is furnished with sparse, stiff hairs, each arising from a tubercle. I have often watched the newly hatched boll while in the cotton fields. When hatched from an egg which had been deposited upon a leaf, they invariably made their first meal on the substance of the leaf, and then wandered about for a longer or shorter space of time, evidently seeking a boll or flower bud. It was always interesting to watch this seemingly aimless search of the young worm, crawling first down the leaf stem and then back, then dropping a few inches by a silken thread and then painfully working its way back again, until, at last, it found the object of its search, or fell to the ground where it was destroyed by ants. As the boll worms increase in size a most wonderful diversity of color and marking becomes apparent. In color different worms will vary from a brilliant green to a deep pink or dark brown, exhibiting almost every conceivable intermediate stage from an immaculate, unstriped specimen to one with regular spots and many stripes. The green worms were more common than those of any other color a common variety was a very light green. When these worms put in an appearance it raised a great excitement among the planters. We did not use any poison to destroy them, as I learn is the method now employed.

## THE COTTON HARVEST.

The cotton harvest, or picking season, began about the latter part of August or first of September, and lasted till Christmas or after, but in the latter part of July picking commenced for "the first bale" to go into the market at Memphis. This picking was done by children from nine to twelve years of age and by women who were known as "sucklers," that is, women with infants. The pickers would pass through the rows getting very little, as the cotton was not yet in full bloom. From the lower part of the stalk where it opened first is where they got the first pickings. The season of first picking was always a great time, for the planter who brought the first bale of cotton into market at Memphis was presented with a basket of champagne by the commission merchants. This was a custom established throughout Mississippi. After the first pickings were secured the cotton developed very fast, continuing to bud and bloom all over the stalk until the frost falls. The season of picking was exciting to all planters, every one was zealous in pushing his slaves in order that he might reap the greatest possible harvest. The planters talked about their prospects, discussed the cotton markets, just as the farmers of the north discuss the markets for their products. I often saw Boss so excited and nervous during the season he scarcely ate. The daily task of each able-bodied slave during the cotton picking season war 250 pounds or more, and all those who did not come up to the required amount would get a whipping. When the planter wanted more cotton picked than usual, the overseer would arrange a race. The slaves would be divided into two parties, with a leader for each party. The first leader would choose a slave for his side, then the second leader one for his, and so on alternately until all were chosen. Each leader tried to get the best on his side. They would all work like good fellows for the prize, which was a tin cup of sugar for each slave on the winning side. The contest was kept up for three days whenever the planter desired an extra amount picked. The slaves were just as interested in the races as if they were going to get a five dollar bill.

PREPARING COTTON FOR MARKET.

The gin-house was situated about four hundred yards from "the great house" on the main road. It was a large shed built upon square timbers, and was similar to a barn, only it stood some six feet from the ground, and underneath was located the machinery for running the gin. The cotton was put into the loft after it was dried, ready for ginning. In this process the cotton was dropped from the loft to the man who fed the machine. As it was ginned the lint would go into the lint room, and the seed would drop at the feeder's feet. The baskets used for holding lint were twice as large as those used in the picking process, and they were never taken from the gin house. These lint baskets were used in removing the lint from the lint room to the place where the cotton was baled. A bale contained 250 pounds, and the man who did the treading of the cotton into the bales would not vary ten pounds in the bale, so accustomed was he to the packing. Generally from fourteen to fifteen bales of cotton were in the lint room at a time.

### OTHER FARM PRODUCTS.

Cotton was the chief product of the Mississippi farms and nothing else was raised to sell. Wheat, oats and rye were raised in limited quantities, but only for the slaves and the stock. All the fine flour for the master's family was bought in St. Louis. Corn was raised in abundance, as it was a staple article of food for the slaves. It was planted about the 1st of March, or about a month earlier than the cotton. It was, therefore, up and partially worked before the cotton was planted and fully tilled before the cotton was ready for cultivation. Peas were planted between the rows of corn, and hundreds of bushels were raised. These peas after being harvested, dried and beaten out of the shell, were of a reddish brown tint, not like those raised for the master's family, but they were considered a wholesome and nutritious food for the slaves. Cabbage and yams, a large sweet potato, coarser than the kind generally used by the whites and not so delicate in flavor, were also raised for the servants in liberal quantities. No hay was raised, but the leaves of the corn, stripped from the stalks while yet green, cured and bound in bundles, were used as a substitute for it in feeding horses.

### FARM IMPLEMENTS.

Almost all the implements used on the plantation were made by the slaves. Very few things were bought. Boss had a skilled blacksmith, uncle Ben, for whom he paid $1,800, and there were slaves who were carpenters and workers in wood who could turn their hands to almost anything. Wagons, plows, harrows, grubbing hoes, hames, collars, baskets, bridle bits and hoe handles were all made on the farm and from the material which it produced, except the iron. The timber used in these implements was generally white or red oak, and was cut and thoroughly seasoned long before it was nedeed. The articles thus manufactured were not fine in form or finish, but they were durable, and answered the purposes of a rude method of agriculture. Horse collars were made from corn husks and from poplar bark which was stripped from the tree, in the spring, when the sap was up and it was soft and pliable, and separated into narrow strips which were plaited together. These collars were easy for the horse, and served the purpose of the more costly leather collar. Every season at least 200 cotton baskets were made. One man usually worked at this all the year round, but in the spring he had three assistants. The baskets were made from oak timber, grown in the home forests and prepared by the slaves. It was no small part of the work of the blacksmith and his assistant to keep the farm implements in good repair, and much of this work was done at night. All the plank used was sawed by hand from timber grown on the master's land, as there were no saw mills in that region. Almost the only things not made on the farm which were in general use there were axes, trace chains and the hoes used in cultivating the cotton.

### THE CLEARING OF NEW LAND.

When additional land was required for cultivation the first step was to go into the forest in summer and "deaden" or girdle the trees on a given tract. This was cutting through the bark all around the trunk about thirty inches from the ground. The trees so treated soon died and in a year or two were in condition to be removed. The season selected for clearing the land was winter, beginning with January. The trees, except the larger ones, were cut down, cut into lengths convenient for handling and piled into great heaps, called "log heaps," and burned. The undergrowth was grubbed out and also piled and burned. The burning was done at night and the sight was often weird and grand. The chopping was done by the men slaves and the grubbing by women. All the trees that blew down during the summer were left as they fell till winter when they were removed. This went on, year after year, until all the trees were cleared out. The first year after the new land was cleared corn was put in, the next season cotton. As a rule corn and cotton were planted alternately, especially if the land was poor, if not, cotton would be continued year after year on the same land. Old corn stalks were always plowed under for the next year's crop and they served as an excellent fertilizer. Cotton was seldom planted on newly cleared land, as the roots and stumps rendered it difficult to cultivate the land without injury to the growing plant.

I never saw women put to the hard work of grubbing until I went to McGee's and I greatly wondered at it. Such work was not done by women slaves in Virginia. Children were required to do some work, it mattered not how many grown people were working. There were always tasks set for the boys and girls ranging in age from nine to thirteen years, beyond these ages they worked with the older slaves. After I had been in Pontotoc two years I had to help plant and hoe, and work in the cotton during the seasons, and soon learned to do everything pertaining to the farm.

### COOKING FOR THE SLAVES.

In summer time the cooking for the slaves was done out of doors. A large fire was built under a tree, two wooden forks were driven into the ground on opposite sides of the fire, a pole laid on the forks and on this kettles were hung over the fire for the preparation of the food. Cabbage and meat, boiled, alternated with meat and peas, were the staple for summer. Bread was furnished with the meals and corn meal dumplings, that is, little balls made of meal and grease from the boiled bacon and dropped into boiling water, were also provided and considered quite palatable, especially if cooked in the water in which the bacon was boiled. In winter the cooking was done in a cabin, and sweet potatoes, dried peas and meat were the principal diet. This bill of fare was for dinner or the mid-day meal. For supper each slave received two pieces of meat and two slices of bread, but these slices were very large, as the loaves were about six inches thick and baked in an old fashioned oven. This bread was made from corn meal for, as I have said, only on holidays and special occasions did the slaves have white bread of any kind. Part of the meat and bread received at supper time was saved for the "morning bite." The slaves never had any breakfast, but went to the field at daylight and after working till the sun was well up, all would stop for their morning bite. Very often some young fellow ate his morning bite the evening before at supper and would have nothing for the morning, going without eating until noon. The stop for morning bite was very short; then all would plunge into work until mid-day, when all hands were summoned to their principal meal.

### CARDING AND SPINNING.

Through the winter and on rainy days in summer, the women of the field had to card the wool and spin it into yarn. They generally worked in pairs, a spinning wheel and cards being assigned to each pair, and while one carded the wool into rolls, the other spun it into yarn suitable for weaving into cloth, or a coarse, heavy thread used in making bridles and lines for the mules that were used in the fields. This work was done in the cabins, and the women working together alternated in the carding and spinning. Four cuts were considered a task or day's work, and if any one failed to complete her task she received a whipping from the madam. At night when the spinners brought their work to the big house I would have it to reel. The reel was a contrivance consisting of a sort of wheel, turned on an axis, used to transfer the yarn from the spools or spindles of the spinning wheels into cuts or hunks. It was turned by hand and when enough yarn had been reeled to make a cut the reel signaled it with a snap. This process was continued until four cuts were reeled which made a hunk, and this was taken off and was ready for use. So the work went on until all was reeled. I often got very weary of this work and would almost fall asleep at it, as it was generally done at night after I had had a long day's toil at something else.

### WEAVING—CLOTHES OF THE SLAVES.

One woman did the weaving and it was her task to weave from nine to ten yards a day. Aunt Liza was our weaver and she was taught the work by the madam. At first she did not get on so well with it and many times I have seen the madam jump at her, pinch and choke her because she was dull in understanding how to do it. The madam made the unreasonable demand that she should do the full task at first, and because she failed she was punished, as was the custom in all cases of failure, no matter how unreasonable the demand. Liza finally became equal to her task and accomplished it each day. But the trouble and worry to me was when I had to assist the madam in warping—getting the work ready for the weaver. She would warp the thread herself and place it in the loom, then I would have to hand her the threads, as she put them through the hames. For any failure in quickly comprehending or doing my work, I did not fail to receive the customary blow, or blows, from her hand.

Each piece of cloth contained forty yards, and this cloth was used in making clothes for the servants. About half of the whole amount required was thus made at home; the remainder was bought, and as it was heavier it was used for winter clothing. Each man was allowed for summer two pairs of pants and two shirts, but no coat. The women had two dresses and two chemises each for summer. For winter the men had each two pairs of pants, one coat, one hat and one pair of coarse shoes. These shoes before being worn had to be greased with tallow, with a little tar in it. It was always a happy time when the men got these winter goods it brought many a smile to their faces, though the supply was meager and the articles of the cheapest. The women's dresses for winter were made of the heavier wool-cloth used for the men. They also had one pair of shoes each and a turban. The women who could utilize old clothes, made for themselves what were called pantalets. They had no stockings or undergarments to protect their limbs—these were never given them. The pantalets were made like a pant-leg, came just above the knee, and were caught and tied. Sometimes they looked well and comfortable. The men's old pant-legs were sometimes used.

I remember once when Boss went to Memphis and brought back a bolt of gingham for turbans for the female slaves. It was a red and yellow check, and the turbans made from it were only to be worn on Sunday. The old women were so glad that they sang and prayed. A little gift from the master was greatly appreciated by them. I always came in for my share each year, but my clothes were somewhat different. I wore pants made of Bosse's old ones, and all his old coats were utilized for me. They rounded them off at the tail just a little and called them jackets. My shoes were not brogans, but made of lighter leather, and made suitable for in the house. I only worked on the farm in busy seasons, and did not have the regular wear of the farm hands. On Monday morning it was a great sight to see all the hands marching to the field. The cotton clothes worn by both men and women, and the turbans of the latter, were snowy white, as were the wool hats of the men—all contrasted with the dark faces of the wearers in a strange and striking manner.

SLAVE MOTHERS—CARE OF THE CHILDREN.

The women who had young babies were assigned to what was considered "light work," such as hoeing potatoes, cutting weeds from the fence corners, and any other work of like character. About nine o'clock in the forenoon, at noon, and three o'clock in the afternoon, these women, known on the farms as "the sucklers," could be seen going from work to nurse their babies. Many were the heart-sighs of these sorrowing mothers as they went to minister to their infants. Sometimes the little things would seem starved, for the mothers could only stop their toil three times a day to care for them. When old enough to receive it, the babies had milk, the liquor from boiled cabbage, and bread and milk together. A woman who was too old to do much of anything was assigned to the charge of these babies in the absence of their mothers. It was rare that she had any one to help her. The cries of these little ones, who were cut off almost entirely from motherly care and protection, were heart-rending.

The cabin used for the infants during the day was a double one, that is, double the usual size, and was located near the great house. The cradles used were made of boards, and were not more than two by three feet in size. The women carried their babies in the cradles to the baby cabin in the morning, taking them to their own cabins at night. The children ranging in age from one to seven years were numerous, and the old woman had them to look after as well as the babies. This was indeed a task, and might well have taxed the strength of a younger woman. They were always from eight to a dozen infants in the cabin. The summer season was trying on the babies and young children. Often they would drink too much liquor from cabbage, or too much buttermilk, and would be taken with a severe colic. I was always called on these occasions to go with Boss to administer medicine. I remember on one occasion a little boy had eaten too much cabbage, and was taken with cramp colic. In a few minutes his stomach was swolen as tight and hard as a baloon, and his teeth clenched. He was given an emetic, put in a mustard bath and was soon relieved. The food was too heavy for these children, and they were nearly always in need of some medical attendance. Excessive heat, with improper food, often brought on cholera infantum, from which the infants sometimes died rapidly and in considerable numbers.

### METHODS OF PUNISHMENT.

The methods of punishment were barbarous in the extreme, and so numerous that I will not attempt to describe them all. One method was to tie the slave to a tree, strip off his clothes, and then whip him with a rawhide, or long, limber switches, or the terrible bull whip. Another was to put the slave in stocks, or to buck him, that is, fasten his feet together, draw up his knees to his chin, tie his hands together, draw them down over the knees, and put a stick under the latter and over the arms. In either of these ways the slave was entirely at the mercy of his tormentors, and the whipping could proceed at their pleasure. After these whippings the slave was often left helpless and bleeding upon the ground, until the master, or overseer, saw fit to let him up. The most common method of punishment was to have the servants form a ring, called the "bull ring," into which the one to be punished was led naked. The slaves were then each given a switch, rawhide, strap or whip, and each one was compelled to cut at the poor victim as he ran around the ring. The ring was composed of men, women and children; and, as they numbered from forty to fifty, each circuit of the ring would result in that number of lashes, and by the time the victim had made two or three rounds his condition can be readily imagined. The overseer was always one of the ring, vigorously using the whip, and seeing that all the slaves did the same. Some of the victims fainted before they had passed once around the ring. Women slaves were punished in the same manner as the men. The salt water bath was given after each punishment. Runaway slaves were usually caught by means of hounds, trained for the purpose by men who made it a business and a source of revenue, notwithstanding its brutal features and degrading influence.

### FOURTH OF JULY BARBECUE.

Barbecue originally meant to dress and roast a hog whole, but has come to mean the cooking of a food animal in this manner for the feeding of a great company. A feast of this kind was always given to us, by Boss, on the 4th of July. The anticipation of it

acted as a stimulant through the entire year. Each
one looked forward to this great day of recreation
with pleasure. Even the older slaves would join in
the discussion of the coming event. It mattered not
what trouble or hardship the year had brought, this
feast and its attendant pleasure would dissipate all
gloom. Some, probably, would be punished on the
morning of the 4th, but this did not matter; the men
thought of the good things in store for them, and
that made them forget that they had been punished.
All the week previous to the great day, the slaves
were in high spirits, the young girls and boys, each
evening, congregating, in front of the cabins, to talk
of the feast, while others would sing and dance.
The older slaves were not less happy, but would only
say: "Ah! God has blessed us in permitting us to
see another feast day." The day before the 4th was
a busy one. The slaves worked with all their might.
The children who were large enough were engaged
in bringing wood and bark to the spot where the
barbecue was to take place. They worked eagerly
all day long; and, by the time the sun was setting,
a huge pile of fuel was beside the trench, ready
use in the morning. At an early hour of the

day, the servants were up, and the men whom Boss had appointed to look after the killing of the hogs and sheep were quickly at their work, and, by the time they had the meat dressed and ready, most of the slaves had arrived at the center of attraction. They gathered in groups, talking, laughing, telling tales that they had from their grandfather, or relating practical jokes that they had played or seen played by others. These tales were received with peals of laughter. But however much they seemed to enjoy these stories and social interchanges, they never lost sight of the trench or the spot where the sweetmeats were to be cooked.

The method of cooking the meat was to dig a trench in the ground about six feet long and eighteen inches deep. This trench was filled with wood and bark which was set on fire, and, when it was burned to a great bed of coals, the hog was split through the back bone, and laid on poles which had been placed across the trench. The sheep were treated in the same way, and both were turned from side to side as they cooked. During the process of roasting the cooks basted the carcasses with a preparation furnished from the great house, consisting of butter, pepper, salt and vinegar, and this was continued until the meat was ready to serve. Not far from this trench were the iron ovens, where the sweetmeats were cooked. Three or four women were assigned to this work. Peach cobbler and apple dumpling were the two dishes that made old slaves smile for joy and the young fairly dance. The crust or pastry of the cobbler was prepared in large earthen bowls, then rolled out like any pie crust, only it was almost twice as thick. A layer of this crust was laid in the oven, then a half peck of peaches poured in, followed by a layer of sugar; then a covering of pastry was laid over all and smoothed around with a knife. The oven was then put over a bed of coals, the cover put on and coals thrown on it, and the process of baking began. Four of these ovens were usually in use at these feasts, so that enough of the pastry might be baked to supply all. The ovens were filled and refilled until there was no doubt about the quantity. The apple dumplings were made in the usual way, only larger, and served with sauce made from brown sugar. It lacked flavoring, such as cinnamon or lemon, yet it was a dish highly relished by all the slaves. I know that these feasts made me so excited,

I could scarcely do my house duties, and I would never fail to stop and look out of the window from the dining room down into the quarters. I was eager to get through with my work and be with the feasters. About noon everything was ready to serve. The table was set in a grove near the quarters, a place set aside for these occasions. The tableware was not fine, being of tin, but it served the purpose, and did not detract from the slaves' relish for the feast. The drinks were strictly temperance drinks — buttermilk and water. Some of the nicest portions of the meat were sliced off and put on a platter to send to the great house for Boss and his family. It was a pleasure for the slaves to do this, for Boss always enjoyed it. It was said that the slaves could barbecue meats best, and when the whites had barbecues slaves always did the cooking. When dinner was all on the table, the invitation was given for all to come; and when all were in a good way eating, Boss and the madam would go out to witness the progress of the feast, and seemed pleased to see the servants so happy. Everything was in abundance, so all could have plenty — Boss always insisted on this. The slaves had the whole day off, and could do as they liked. After dinner some of the women would wash, sew or iron. It was a day of harmless riot for all the slaves, and I can not express the happiness it brought them. Old and young, for months, would rejoice in the memory of the day and its festivities, and "bless" Boss for this ray of sunlight in their darkened lives.

### ATTENDANCE AT CHURCH.

There was an observance of religious forms at least by the occupants of both the great house and the cabins. The McGee family were church-going people, and, except in very inclement weather, never failed to attend service on Sunday. They were Methodists, and their church was four miles from their residence. The Baptist church was but two miles distant, and the family usually alternated in their attendance between the two places of worship. I always attended them to church, generally riding behind while the Boss drove. Upon reaching church, my first duty was to run to a spring for a pitcher of fresh water, which I passed not only to the members of our party, but to any others desiring drink. Whatever may be thought of the religious professions of the slave-holders, there can be no question that many of the slaves were sincere believers in the

Christian religion, and endeavored to obey the precepts according to their light.

## RELIGIOUS MEETINGS OF THE SLAVES.

Saturday evening on the farm was always hailed with delight. The air was filled with happy shouts from men and boys, so glad were they that Sunday, their only day of rest, was near. In the cabins the women were washing and fixing garments for Sunday, that they might honor the Lord in cleanliness and decency. It was astonishing how they utilized what they had, and with what skill and industry they performed these self-imposed tasks. Where the family was large it was often after midnight before this work was done. While this preparation for the Sabbath was in progress in most of the cabins, the old men would gather in one for a prayer-meeting. As they began to sing some familiar hymn, the air would ring with their voices, and it was not long before the cabin was filled with both old and young, who came in their simple yet sincere way to give praise to God. It was common to have one or two colored men on the plantation who claimed to be called to preach God, by teaching their fellow men the principles of religion. God certainly must have revealed himself to these poor souls, for they were very ignorant—they did not know a letter of the Bible. But when they opened their mouths they were filled, and the plan of Salvation was explained in a way that all could receive it. It was always a mystery to the white brethren how the slaves could line out hymns, preach Christ and redemption, yet have no knowledge even of how the name of Christ was spelled. They were illiterate to the last degree, so there is but one theory, they were inspired. God revealed unto them just what they should teach their flock, the same as he did to Moses. I remember very well that there was always a solemnity about the services — a certain harmony, which had a peculiar effect — a certain pathetic tone which quickened the emotions as they sang those old plantation hymns. It mattered not what their troubles had been during the week — how much they had been lashed, the prayer-meeting on Saturday evening never failed to be held. Their faith was tried and true. On Sunday afternoons, they would all congregate again to praise God, and the congregation was enthusiastic. It was pathetic to hear them pray, from the depths of their hearts, for them who "despitefully used them and persecuted them." This injunction of our Saviour was strictly adhered to. The words that came from the minister were always of a consolatory kind. He knew the crosses of his fellow slaves and their hardships, for he had shared them himself. I was always touched in hearing him give out the hymns. I can hear old Uncle Ben now, as he solemnly worded out the following lines:

>Must I be carried to the skies,
>On flowery beds of ease,
>While others fought to win the prize,
>And sailed through bloody seas?

After singing he would always speak to them of the necessity for patience in bearing the crosses, urging them to endure "as good soldiers." Many tears were shed, and many glad shouts of praise would burst forth during the sermon. A hymn usually followed the sermon, then all retired. Their faces seemed to shine with a happy light their very countenances showed that their souls had been refreshed and that it had been "good for them to be there." These meetings were the joy and comfort of the slaves, and even those who did not profess Christianity were calm and thoughtful while in attendance.

## A NEIGHBORHOOD QUARREL.

Opposite our farm was one owned by a Mr. Juval, and adjoining that was another belonging to one White. The McGees and the Whites were very fast friends, visiting each other regularly—indeed they had grown up together, and Mr. White at one time was the lover of the madam, and engaged to be married to her. This friendship had existed for years, when McGee bought the Juval farm, for which White had also been negotiating, but which he failed to get on account of McGee having out-bid him. From this circumstance ill feeling was engendered between the two men, and they soon became bitter enemies. McGee had decided to build a fence between the farm he had purchased and that of White, and, during the winter, his teamsters were set to hauling the rails; and, in unloading them, they accidently threw some of them over the line on to White's land. The latter said nothing about the matter until spring, when he wrote McGee a letter, asking him to remove the rails from his land. McGee paid no attention to the request, and he soon received a second note, when he said to his wife: "That fellow is about to turn himself a fool—I'll give him a cow-hiding." A third and more emphatic note followed, in which White told the Boss that the rails must be removed within twenty-four hours. He grew indignant, and, in true Southern style, he went immediately to town and bought arms, and prepared himself for the fray. When he returned he had every hand on the plantation stop regular work, and put them all to building the fence. I was of the number. Boss and the overseer came out to overlook the work and hurry it on. About four o'clock in the afternoon White put in an appearance, and came face to face with McGee, sitting on his horse and having a double barreled shot gun lying across the pummel of his saddle. White passed on without saying a word, but Boss yelled at him: "Hello! I see you are about to turn yourself into a fool." White checked up and began to swear, saying: "You are a coward to attack an unarmed man." He grew furious, took off his hat, ran his fingers through his hair, saying: "Here I am, blow me up, and I'll have some one blow you there be-fore night." During White's rage he said: "I'll fight you anywhere—bowie-knife fight, shot gun fight or any other." He called, in his excitement, for his men who were working on his farm, to come, and immediately sent him to Billy Duncan's to get him a double barreled shot gun. Meantime, Mrs. McGee appeared on the scene, and began to cry, begging White to stop and allow her to speak to him. But he replied: "Go off, go off, I don't want to speak to you." Boss grew weak and sick, and through his excitement, was taken violently ill, vomiting as if he had taken an emetic. He said to White: "I'll return as soon as I take my wife home," but he never came back. As Boss and the madam rode off, White came galloping back, and said to Brooks, our overseer: "If I am shot down on foul play would you speak of it?" Brooks replied: "No, I don't care to interfere—I don't wish to have anything to do with it." White was bloodthirsty, and came back at intervals during the entire night, where we were working, to see if he could find Boss. It is quite probable that White may have long cherished a secret grudge against Boss, because he had robbed him of his first love; and, brooding over these offenses, he became so excited as to be almost insane. Had McGee returned that night, White would certainly have shot him. Boss became so uneasy over the situation that he sent one of his slaves, a foreman, to Panola county, some seventy-five miles distant, to Mrs. McGee's father, to get her brother, a lawyer, to come and endeavor to effect a settlement. He came, but all his efforts were unavailing. The men met at a magistrate's office, but they came to no understanding. Our folks became dissatisfied, and did not care to remain longer in the place, so they began to look out for other quarters. Boss finally decided to buy a farm in Bolivar, Miss., and to remove his family to Memphis, where he secured a fine place, just outside of the city.

# CHAPTER II.

## SOCIAL AND OTHER ASPECTS OF SLAVERY.

### REMOVAL TO MEMPHIS, TENNESSEE.

McGee had decided to build a new house upon the property which he had purchased at Memphis; and, in August 1850, he sent twenty-five of his slaves to the city, to make brick for the structure, and I went along as cook. After the bricks were burned, the work of clearing the ground for the buildings was commenced. There were many large and beautiful trees that had to be taken up and removed; and, when this work was completed, the excavations for the foundations and the cellar were undertaken. All of this work was done by the slaves. The site was a beautiful one, embracing fourteen acres, situated two miles southeast from the city, on the Memphis and Charleston railroad. The road ran in front of the place and the Boss built a flag-station there, for the accommodation of himself and his neighbors, which was named McGee Station.

## A NEW AND SPLENDID HOUSE.

The house was one of the most pretentious in that region, and was a year and a half in building. It was two stories in height, and built of brick, the exterior surface being coated with cement and marked off in blocks, about two feet square, to represent stone. It was then whitewashed. There was a veranda in front with six large columns, and, above, a balcony. On the back there were also a veranda and a balcony, extending across that end to the servants' wing. A large hall led from front to rear, on one side of which were double parlors, and on the other a sitting room, a bedroom and a dining room. In the second story were a hall and four rooms, similar in all respects to those below, and above these was a large attic. The interior woodwork was of black walnut. The walls were white, and the center-pieces in the ceilings of all the rooms were very fine, being the work of an English artisan, who had been for a short time in this country. This work was so superior in design and finish, to anything before seen in that region that local artisans were much excited over it, and some offered to purchase the right to produce it, but Boss refused the offer. However, some one, while the house was finishing, helped himself to the design, and it was reproduced, in whole or in part, in other buildings in the city. This employment of a foreign artist was unusual there and caused much comment. The parlors were furnished with mahogany sets, the upholstering being in red brocade satin. The dining room was also furnished in mahogany. The bedrooms had mahogany bedsteads of the old-fashioned pattern with canopies. Costly bric-a-brac, which Boss and the madam had purchased while traveling in foreign countries, was in great profusion. Money was no object to Edmund McGee, and he added every modern improvement and luxury to his home; the decorations and furnishings were throughout of the most costly and elegant; and in the whole of Tennessee there was not a mansion more sumptuously complete in all its appointments, or more palatial in its general appearance. When all was finished — pictures, bric-a-brac, statuary and flowers all in their places, Mrs. McGee was brought home.

In this new house Boss opened up in grand style; everything was changed, and the family entered upon a new, more formal and more pretentious manner of living. I was known no longer as errand boy, but installed as butler and body-servant to my master. I had the same routine of morning work, only it was more extensive. There was a great deal to be done in so spacious a mansion. Looking after the parlors, halls and dining rooms, arranging flowers in the rooms, waiting on the table, and going after the mail was my regular morning work, the year round. Then there were my duties to perform, night and morning, for my master; these were to brush his clothes, black his shoes, assist him to arrange his toilet, and do any little thing that he wanted me to. Aside from these regular duties, there were windows to wash, silver to polish and steps to stone on certain days in the week. I was called to do any errand neccessary, and sometimes to assist in the garden. A new staff of house servants was installed, as follows: Aunt Delia, cook; Louisa, chambermaid; Puss, lady's maid to wait on the madam; Celia, nurse; Lethia, wet nurse; Sarah, house maid; Julia, laundress; Uncle Gooden, gardener; Tom, coachman.

### NEW STYLE OF LIVING.

I was, at first, dazed with the splendor of the place, and laughed and chuckled to themselves a good deal about mars' fine house, and really seemed pleased; for, strange to say, the slaves of rich people always rejoiced in that fact. A servant owned by a man in moderate circumstances was hooted at by rich men's slaves. It was common for them to say: "Oh! don't mind that darkey, he belongs to po'r white trash." So, as I said, our slaves rejoiced in master's good luck. Each of the women servants wore a new, gay colored turban, which was tied differently from that of the ordinary servant, in some fancy knot. Their frocks and aprons were new, and really the servants themselves looked new. My outfit was a new cloth suit, and my aprons for wearing when waiting on the table were of snowy white linen, the style being copied from that of the New York waiters. I felt big, for I never knew what a white bosom shirt was before; and even though the grief at the separation from my dear mother was almost unbearable at times, and my sense of loneliness in having no relative near me often made me sad, there was consolation, if not compensation, in this little change. I had known no comforts, and had been so cowed and broken in spirits, by cruel lashings, that I really felt light-hearted at this improvement in my personal appearance, although it was merely for the gratification of my master's pride; and I thought I would do all I could to please Boss.

### THE ADORNMENT OF THE GROUNDS.

For some time before all the appointments of the new home were completed, a great number of mechanics and workmen, besides our own servants, were employed; and there was much bustle and stir about the premises. Considerable out-door work was yet to be done—fences to be made, gardens and orchards to be arranged and planted, and the grounds about the house to be laid out and adorned with shubbery and flower beds. When this work was finally accomplished, the grounds were indeed beautiful. The walks were graveled, and led through a profusion of shrubbery and flower beds. There was almost every variety of roses; while, scattered over the grounds, there were spruce, pine and juniper trees, and some rare varieties, seldom seen in this northern climate. Around the grounds was set a cedar hedge, and, in time, the place became noted for the beauty of its shrubbery; the roses especially were marvelous in the richness and variety of their colors, their fragrance and the luxuriousness of their growth. People who have never traveled in the South have little idea of the richness and profusion of its flowers, especially of its roses. Among the climbing plants, which adorned the house, the most beautiful and fragrant was the African honeysucle—its ordor was indeed delightful.

### THE GARDEN.

One of the institutions of the place was the vegetable garden. This was established not only for the convenience and comfort of the family, but to furnish employment for the slaves. Under the care of Uncle Gooden, the gardner, it flourished greatly; and there was so much more produced than the family could use, Boss concluded to sell the surplus. The gardner, therefore, went to the city, every morning, with a load of vegetables, which brought from eight to ten dollars daily, and this the madam took for "pin money." In the spring I had always to help the gardner in setting out plants and preparing beds; and, as this was in connection with my other work, I became so tired sometimes that I could hardly stand. All the vegetables raised were fine, and at that time brought a good price. The first cabbage that we sold in the markets brought twenty-five cents a head. The first sweet potatoes marketed always brought a dollar a peck, or four dollars a bushel. The Memphis market regulations required that all vegetables be washed before being exposed for sale. Corn was husked, and everything was clean and inviting. Any one found guilty of selling, or exhibiting for sale, vegetables of a previous day was fined, at once, by the market master. This rule was carried out to the letter. Nothing stale could be sold, or even come into market. The rules required that all poultry be dressed before being brought to market. The entrails were cleaned and strung and sold separately—usually for about ten cents a string.

### PROFUSION OF FLOWERS.

Flowers grew in profusion everywhere through the south, and it has, properly, been called the land of flowers. But flowers had no such sale there as have our flowers here in the north. The pansy and many of our highly prized plants and flowers grew wild in the south. The people there did not seem to care for flowers as we do. I have sold many bouquets for a dime, and very beautiful ones for fifteen and twenty cents, that would sell in the north for fifty to seventy-five cents.

### THE FRUIT ORCHARD.

The new place had an orchard of about four acres, consisting of a variety of apple, peach, pear and plum trees. Boss hired an expert gardner to teach me the art of grafting, and, after some practice, I became quite skilled in this work. Some of the pear trees that had been grafted had three different kinds of fruit on them, and others had three kinds of apples on them besides the pears. This grafting I did myself, and the trees were considered very fine by Boss. Another part of my work was the trimming of the hedge and the care of all the shrubbery.

### I PRACTICE MEDICINE AMONG THE SLAVES.

McGee had a medicine chest built into the wall of the new house. The shelves for medicine were of wood, and the arrangement was very convenient. It was really a small drug store. It contained everything in the way of drugs that was necessary to use in doctoring the slaves. We had quinine, castor-oil, alcohol and ipecac in great quantities, as these were the principal drugs used in the limited practice in the home establishment. If a servant came from the field to the house with a chill, which was frequent, the first thing we did was to give him a dose of ipecac to vomit him. On the evening after, we would give him two or three of Cook's pills. These pills we made at home, I always had to prepare the medicines, and give the dose, the Boss standing by dictating. Working with medicine, giving it and caring for the sick were the parts of my work that I liked best. Boss used Dr. Gunn's book altogether for recipes in putting up medicines. He read me the recipe, while I compounded it.

### A SWELL RECEPTION.

In celebration of the opening of the new house, McGee gave an elaborate reception and dinner. The menu embraced nearly everything that one could think of or desire, and all in the greatest profusion. It was a custom, not only with the McGees but among the southern people generally, to make much of eating — it was one of their hobbies. Everything was cooked well, and highly seasoned. Scarcity was foreign to the homes of the wealthy southerners.

### RELATIVES VISIT AT THE MANSION.

After the family had been settled about a month in the new home, their relatives in Panola Co., Miss., Mr. Jack McGee, known among the servants as "Old

Jack," Mrs. Melinda McGee, his wife, Mrs. Farrington, their daughter who was a widow, and their other children Louisa, Ella and William, all came up for a visit, and to see the wonderful house. Mr. Jack McGee was the father of madam and the uncle of Boss. My master and mistress were therefore first cousins, and Boss sometimes called the old man father and at other times, uncle. Old Master Jack, as he alighted, said to those behind him: "Now be careful, step lightly, Louisa, this is the finest house you ever set foot in." When all had come into the house, and the old man had begun to look around, he said: "I don't know what Edmund is thinking about-out to build such a house-house." He was very old, and had never lost all of his Scotch dialect, and he had a habit of repeating a part or all of some words, as in the foregoing quotation. The other members of the visiting family were well pleased with the house, and said it was grand. They laughed and talked merrily over the many novel things which they saw. Mrs. Farrington, who was a gay widow, was naturally interested in everything. I busied myself waiting upon them, and it was late that night before I was through. So many made extra work for me.

### ONE OF THE VISITORS DISTRUSTS ME.

The next morning, after breakfast, Boss and old Master Jack went out to view the grounds. They took me along so that if anything was wanted I could do it. Boss would have me drive a stake in some place to mark where he desired to put something, perhaps some flowers, or a tree. He went on through the grounds, showing his father how everything was to be arranged. The old man shook his head, and said: "Well, it's good, but I am afraid you'll spoil these niggers-niggers. Keep you eye on that boy Lou, (meaning me) he is slippery-slippery, too smart-art." "Oh! I'll manage that, Father," said Boss. "Well, see that you do-oo, for I see running away in his eyes." One of the things that interested old Master Jack was the ringing of the dinner bell. "Well, I do think," said the old man, "that boy can ring a bell better than anbody I ever heard. Why, its got a regular tune." I used to try to see how near I could come to making it say, come to dinner.

### THE MADAM IN A RAGE.

The four days soon passed, and all the company gone, we were once more at our regular work. Delia, the cook, seemingly had not pleased the madam in her cooking while the company were there; so, the morning after they left, she went toward the kitchen, calling: "Delia, Delia." Delia said: "Dah! I wonder what she wants now." By this time she was in the kitchen, confronting Delia. Her face was flushed as she screamed out: "What kind of biscuits were those you baked this week?" "I think they were all right, Mis Sarh." "Hush!" screamed out the madam, stamping her foot to make it more emphatic. "You did not half cook them," said she; "they were not beat enough. Those waffles were ridiculous," said the madam. "Well, Mis Sarh, I tried." "Stop!" cried Madam in a rage, "I'll give you thunder if you dictate to me." Not a very elegant display in language or manner for a great lady! Old Aunt Delia, who was used to these occurances, said: "My Lord! dat woman dunno what she wants. Ah! Lou, there is nothing but the devil up here, (meaning the new home); can't do nothin to please her up here in dis fine house. I tell you Satan neber git his own til he git her." They did not use baking powder, as we do now, but the biscuits were beaten until light enough. Twenty minutes was the time allotted for this work; but when company came there was so much to be done — so many more dishes to prepare, that Delia would, perhaps, not have so much time for each meal. But there was no allowance made. It was never thought reasonable that a servant should make a mistake — things must always be the same. I was listening to this quarrel between madam and Delia, supposing my time would come next; but for that once she said nothing to me.

### THE MADAM'S SEVERITY.

Mrs. McGee was naturally irritable. Servants always got an extra whipping when she had any personal trouble, as though they could help it. Every morning little Kate, Aunt Delia's little girl, would have to go with the madam on her rounds to the different buildings of the establishment, to carry the key basket. So many were the keys that they were kept in a basket especially provided for them, and the child was its regular bearer. The madam, with this little attendant, was everywhere—in the barn, in the hennery, in the smokehouse—and she always made trouble with the servants wherever she went. Indeed, she rarely returned to the house from these rounds without having whipped two or three servants, whether there was really any cause for the punishment or not. She seldom let a day pass without beating some poor woman unmercifully. The number and severity of these whippings depended more upon the humor of the madam than upon the conduct of the slaves. Of course, I always came in for a share in this brutal treatment. She continued her old habit of boxing my jaws, pinching my ears; no day ever passing without her indulging in this exercise of her physical powers. So long had I endured this, I came to expect it, no matter how well I did my duties; and it had its natural effect upon me, making me a coward, even though I was now growing into manhood. I remember once, in particular, when I had tried to please her by arranging the parlor, I overheard her say: "They soon get spirit—it don't do to praise servants." My heart sank within me. What good was it for me to try to please? She would find fault anyway. Her usual morning greeting was: "Well, Lou, have you dusted the parlors?" "Oh, yes," I would answer. "Have the flowers been arranged?" "Yes, all is in readiness," I would say. Once I had stoned the steps as usual, but the madam grew angry as soon as she saw them. I had labored hard, and thought she would be pleased. The result, however, was very far from that. She took me out, stripped me of my shirt and began thrashing me, saying I was spoiled. I was no longer a child, but old enough to be treated differently. I began to cry, for it seemed to me my heart would break. But, after the first burst of tears, the feeling came over me that I was a man, and it was an outrage to treat me so—to keep me under the lash day after day.

### A SHOCKING ACCIDENT.

Not long after Mrs. Farrington had made her first visit to our house, she came there to live. Celia had been acting as her maid. When Mrs. Farrington had been up some months, it was decided that all the family should go down to old Master Jack's for a visit. Celia, the maid, had been so hurried in the preparations for this visit that she had done nothing for herself. The night before the family was to leave, therefore, she was getting ready a garment for herself to wear on the trip; and it was supposed that she sewed until midnight, or after, when she fell asleep, letting the goods fall into the candle. All at once, a little after twelve o'clock, I heard a scream, then a cry of "fire! fire!" and Boss yelling: "Louis! Louis!" I jumped up, throwing an old coat over me, and ran up stairs, in the direction of Mrs. Farrington's room, I encountered Boss in the hall; and, as it was dark and the smoke stifling, I could hardly make any headway. At this moment Mrs. Farrington threw her door open, and screemed for "Cousin Eddie," meaning McGee. He hurriedly called to me to get a pitcher of water quick. I grasped the pitcher from the stand, and he attempted to throw the water on Celia, who was all in a blaze, running around like a mad woman; but the pitcher slipped from his hand and broke, very little of the water reaching her. She was at last wrapped in an old blanket, to extinguish the flames; but she was burned too badly to recover. Boss, being a physician, said at once: "Poor girl, poor girl! she is burned to death." He did all he could for her, wrapped her in linen sheets, and endeavored to relieve her sufferings, but all was of no avail—she had inhaled the flame, injuring her internally, and lived only a few days.

MASTER'S NEW COTTON PLANTATION.

Shortly after Boss bought his home in Memphis, he bought a large farm in Bolivar, Miss. It was a regular cotton farm, on the Missippi river, embracing 200 acres. The houses built for the slaves were frame, eighteen in number, each to contain three or four families, and arranged on each side of a street that ran through the farm. This street was all grassed over, but there were no sidewalks. All the buildings —the barn, gin-house, slaves' quarters and overseers' house were whitewashed, and on this grass-grown street they made a neat and pretty appearance. The house where the Boss and the madam staid, when they went down to the farm, was about two hundred yards from the slaves' quarters. It was arranged in two appartments, one for the overseer and wife, and the other for the master and mistress upon the occasion of their visits. This building was separated from the other buildings by a fence. There was what was called the cook house, where was cooked all the food for the hands. Aunt Matilda was cook in charge. Besides the buildings already named, there were stables, a blacksmith shop and sawmill; and the general order of arrangement was carried out with respect to all the appearance was that of a village. Everything was raised in abundance, to last from one crop to the next. Vegetables and meat were provided from the farm, and a dairy of fifty cows furnished all the milk and butter needed.

The cane brakes were so heavy that it was common for bears to hide there, and, at night, come out and carry off hogs. Wolves were plenty in the woods behind the farm, and could be heard at any time. The cane was so thick that when they were clearing up new ground, it would have to be set on fire, and the cracking that would ensue was like the continuous explosion of small fire crackers.

About one hundred and sixty slaves, besides children, all owned by McGee, were worked on the farm. Instead of ginning two or three bales of cotton a day, as at Pontotoc, they ginned six to seven bales here.

### INCIDENTS.

I remember well the time when the great Swedish singer, Jenny Lind, came to Memphis. It was during her famous tour through America, in 1851. Our folks were all enthused over her. Boss went in and secured tickets to her concert, and I was summoned to drive them to the hall. It was a great event. People swarmed the streets like bees. The carriages and hacks were stacked back from the hall as far as the eye could reach.

On another occasion, when the great prodigy,

Blind Tom, came to Memphis, there was a similar stir among the people. Tom was very young then, and he was called the Blind Boy. People came from far and near to hear him. Those coming from the villages and small towns, who could not get passage on the regular trains, came in freight or on flat bottom cars. The tickets were $5.00 each, as I remember, Boss said it was expensive, but all must hear this boy pianist. Many were the comments on this boy of such wonderful talents. As I drove our people home they seemed to talk of nothing else. They declared that he was indeed a wonder.

### LONGING FOR FREEDOM.

Sometimes when the farm hands were at work, peddlers would come along; and, as they were treated badly by the rich planters, they hated them, and talked to the slaves in a way to excite them and set them thinking of freedom. They would say encouragingly to them: "Ah! You will be free some day." But the down-trodden slaves, some of whom were bowed with age, with frosted hair and furrowed cheek, would answer, looking up from their work: "We don't blieve dat; my grandfather said we was to be free, but we aint free yet." It had been talked of (this freedom) from generation to generation. Perhaps they would not have thought of freedom, if their owners had not been so cruel. Had my mistress been more kind to me, I should have thought less of liberty. I know the cruel treatment which I received was the main thing that made me wish to be free. Besides this, it was inhuman to separate families as they did. Think of a mother being sold from all her children — separated for life! This separation was common, and many died heart-broken, by reason of it. Ah! I cannot forget the cruel separation from my mother. I know not what became of her, but I have always believed her dead many years ago. Hundreds were separated, as my mother and I were, and never met again. Though freedom was yearned for by some because the treatment was so bad, others, who were bright and had looked into the matter, knew it was a curse to be held a slave — they longed to stand out in true manhood — allowed to express their opinions as were white men. Others still desired freedom, thinking they could then reclaim a wife, or husband, or children. The mother would again see her child. All these promptings of the heart made them yearn for freedom. New Year's was always a heart-rending time, for it was then the slaves were bought and sold; and they stood in constant fear of losing some one dear to them — a child, a husband, or wife.

### MY FIRST BREAK FOR FREEDOM.

In the new home my duties were harder than ever. The McGees held me with tighter grip, and it was nothing but cruel abuse, from morning till night. So I made up my mind to try and run away to a free country. I used to hear Boss read sometimes, in the papers, about runaway slaves who had gone to Canada, and it always made me long to go; yet I never appeared as if I paid the slightest attention to what the family read or said on such matters; but I felt that I could be like others, and try at least to get away. One morning, when Boss had gone to town, Madam had threatened to whip me, and told me to come to the house. When she called me I did not go, but went off down through the garden and through the woods, and made my way for the city. When I got into Memphis, I found at the landing a boat called the Statesman, and I sneaked aboard. It was not expected that the boat would stay more than a few hours, but, for some reason, it stayed all night.

The boat was loaded with sugar, and I hid myself behind four hogsheads. I could see both engineers, one each side of me. When night came on, I crept out from my hiding place, and went forward to search for food and water, for I was thirsty and very hungry. I found the table where the deck hands had been eating, and managed to get a little food, left from their meal, and some water. This was by no means enough, but I had to be content, and went back to my place of concealment. I had been on board the boat three days; and, on the third night, when I came out to hunt food, the second mate saw me. In a minute he eyed me over and said: "Why, I have a reward for you." In a second he had me go up stairs to the captain. This raised a great excitement among the passengers; and, in a minute, I was besieged with numerous questions. Some spoke as if they were sorry for me, and said if they had known I was a poor runaway slave they would have slipped me ashore. The whole boat was in alarm. It seemed to me they were consulting slips of paper. One said: "Yes, he is the same. Listen how this reads:"

"Ran away from Edmund McGee, my mulatto boy Louis, 5 feet 6 inches in height, black hair, is very bright and intelligent. Will give $500 for him alive, and half of this amount for knowledge that he has been killed."

My heart sprang into my throat when I heard two men read this advertisement. I knew, at once, what it all meant, remembering how often I had heard Boss read such articles from the papers and from the handbills that were distributed through the city. The captain asked me if I could dance. It seemed he felt sorry for me, for he said: "That's a bright boy to be a slave." Then turning to me he said: "Come, give us a dance." I was young and nimble, so I danced a few of the old southern clog dances, and sang one or two songs, like this:

"Come along, Sam, the fifer's son,
Aint you mighty glad your day's work's done?"

After I finished singing and dancing, the captain took up a collection for me and got about two dollars. This cheered me a good deal. I knew that I would need money if I should ever succeed in getting on.

On the following evening, when we reached West Franklin, Indiana, while the passengers were at tea, another boat pushed into port right after ours. Immediately a gentleman passenger came to me hurriedly, and whispered to me to go down stairs, jump out on the bow of the other boat, and go ashore. I was alarmed, but obeyed, for I felt that he was a friend to slaves. I went out as quietly as I could, and was not missed until I had gotten on shore. Then I heard the alarm given that the boy was gone -- that the runaway was gone. But I sped on, and did not stop until I had run through the village, and had come to a road that led right into the country. I took this road and went on until I had gone four or five miles, when I came to a farm house. Before reaching it, however, I met two men on horseback, on their way to the village. They passed on without specially noticing me, and I kept on my way until reaching the farmhouse. I was so hungry, I went in and asked for food. While I was eating, the men whom I had met rode up. They had been to the village, and, learning that a runaway slave was wanted, and remembering meeting me, they returned in hot haste, in hope of finding me and securing the reward. They hallooed to the people in the house, an old woman and her daughter, whom they seemed to know, saying: "There is a runaway nigger out, who stole off a boat this evening." The old lady said, "Come," becoming frightened at once. When they came in they began to question me. I trembled all over but answered them. They said: "You are the fellow we want, who ran off the boat." I was too scared to deny it; so I owned I was on the boat, and stole off. They did not tarry long, but, taking me with them, they went, about a mile and a half, to their house. They planned and talked all the way, and one said: "We are good for $75.00 for him any way." The next morning they took me into the village. They soon found out that the engineer, by order of the captain, had stayed over to search for me. A lawsuit followed, and I was taken before the magistrate before the engineer could get possession of me. There was a legal course that had to be gone through with. A lawyer, Fox by name, furnished the $75.00 for the men who had caught me. That part of the case being settled, Fox and the engineer started for Evansville, Ind., that same night. Upon arriving there, Fox received from the captain of the boat the money he had advanced to the men who caught me; and we went on, arriving at Louisville, Ky., the next day. I was then taken again before a magistrate, by the captain, when the following statement was read by that official:

"Captain Montgomery brought forth a boy, and said he is the property of Edmund McGee, of Memphis, Tenn. Come forth owner, and prove property, for after the boy shall remain in jail six months he shall be sold to pay jail feed."

Mr. McGee was informed of my whereabouts, and it was not long before he and his cousin came to get me. When they came, I was called up by the nickname they had given me, "Memphis." "Come out here, 'Memphis,'" said the turnkey, "your master has come for you." I went down stairs to the office, and found Boss waiting for me. "Hello, Lou!" said he, "what are you doing here, you dog?" I was so frightened I said nothing. Of course, some few words were passed between him and the officers. I heard him say that I was a smart fellow, and he could not tell why I had run away; that he had always treated me well. This was to impress the officers with the idea that he was not unkind to his slaves. The slave-holders all hated to be classed as bad taskmasters. Yet nearly all of them were. The clothes I wore were jail property, and he could not take me away in them; so we started to go up town to get others. As we passed out the jailor, Buckhanon, said: "Ain't you going to put hand-cuffs on him?" "Oh, no!" said Boss. After I was taken to the store and fitted with a new suit of clothes, he brought me back to the jail, where I washed myself and put on the new garments. When all was complete, and I seemed to suit master's fastidious eye, he took me to the Gault House, where he was stopping. In the evening we started for home, and reached Memphis the following day. Boss did not flog me, as I expected, but sent me to my regular routine work. We had been in this new home so short a time he did not want it to be rumored that he whipped his slaves, he was so stylish and rich. But the madam was filled with rage, although she did not say much. I think they saw that I was no longer a child - they feared I would go again. But after I had been home some three or four weeks, Madam Sarah commenced her old tricks attempting to whip me, box my jaws and pinch me. If any little thing was not pleasing to her at meal time, it was a special delight for her to reach out, when I drew near to her to pass something, and give me a blow with her hand. Truly it was a monstrous domestic institution that not only tolerated, but fostered, such an exhibition of table manners by a would-be fine lady--such vulgar spite and cruelty!

## MY SECOND RUNAWAY TRIP.

About three months after my first attempt to get away, I thought I would try it again. I went to Memphis, and saw a boat at the landing, called the John Lirozey, a Cincinnati packet. This boat carried the mail. She had come into port in the morning, and was being unloaded. I went aboard in the afternoon and jumped down into the hull. Boss had been there in the fore part of the afterooon inquiring for me, but I did not know it then. After I had been in the boat some time, the men commenced loading it. I crept up in the corner and hid myself. At first two or three hundred dry and green hides were thrown in, and these hid me; but later on two or three tiers of cotton bales were put in the center of the hull, and, when the boat started, I got upon the top of these, and lay there. I could hear the people talking above me, but it was so dark I could not see anything— it was dark as a dungeon. I had lain there two nights and began to get so weak and faint I could stand it no longer. For some reason the boat did not start the day I went aboard, consequently, I had not gotten as far from home as I expected, and my privations had largely been in vain. Despairing and hungry, on the third day, I commenced howling and screaming, hoping that some one would hear me, and come to my relief, for almost anything else would have been preferable to the privation and hunger from which I was suffering. But I could make no one hear, at least no one paid any attention to my screams, if they did hear. In the evening, however, one of the deck hands came in with a lantern to look around and see everything was all right. I saw the light and followed him out, but I had been out of my hiding only a short time when I was discovered by a man who took me up stairs to the captain. It was an effort for me to walk up stairs, as I was weak and faint, having neither eaten nor drank anything for three days. This boat was crowded with passengers, and it was soon a scene of confusion. I was placed in the pilot's room for safety, until we arrived at a small town in Kentucky called Monroe. I was put off here to be kept until the packet came back from Cincinnati. Then I was carried back to Memphis, arriving about one o'clock at night, and, for safe keeping, was put into what was called the calaboose. This was especially for the keeping of slaves who had run away and been caught. Word was sent to Boss of my capture; and the next morning Thomas Bland, a fellow servant of mine, was sent to take me home. I can not tell how I felt, for the only thought that came to me was that I should get killed. The madam met us as we drove into the yard. "Ah!" she said to me, "you put up at the wrong hotel, sir." I was taken to the barn where stocks had been prepared, beside which were a cowhide and a pail of salt water, all prepared for me. It was terrible, but there was no escape. I was fastened in the stocks, my clothing removed, and the whipping began. Boss whipped me a while, then he sat down and read his paper, after which the whipping was resumed. This continued for two hours. Fastened as I was in the stocks, I could only stand and take lash after lash, as long as he desired, the terrible rawhide cutting into my flesh at every stroke. Then he used peach tree switches, which cracked the flesh so the blood oozed out. After this came the paddle, two and a half feet long and three inches wide. Salt and water was at once applied to wash the wounds, and the smarting was maddening. This torture was common among the southern planters. God only knows what I suffered under it all, and He alone gave me strength to endure it. I could hardly move after the terrible ordeal was finished, and could scarcely bear my clothes to touch me at first, so sore was my whole body, and it was weeks before I was myself again.

### PREACHING TO THE SLAVES.

As an offset, probably, to such diabolical cruelties as those which were practiced upon me in common with nearly all the slaves in the cotton region of the south, it was the custom in the section of country where I lived to have the white minister preach to the servants Sunday afternoon, after the morning service for the whites. The white people hired the minister by the year to preach for them at their church. Then he had to preach to each master's slaves in turn. The circuit was made once a month, but there was service of some kind every Sunday. The slaves on some places gathered in the yard, at others in the white folks' school houses, and they all seemed pleased and eager to hear the word of God. It was a strong evidence of their native intelligence and discrimination that they could discern the difference between the truths of the "word" and the professed practice of those truths by their masters. My Boss took pride in having all his slaves look clean any tidy at the Sabbath service; but how would he have liked to have the slaves, with backs lacerated with the lash, appear in those assemblies with their wounds uncovered? The question can never be answered. The master and most of his victims have gone where professions of righteousness will not avail to cover the barbarities practised here.

A FAMILY OF FREE PERSONS SOLD INTO SLAVERY.

My wife Matilda was born in Fayette county, Kentucky, June 17th, 1830. It seems that her mother and her seven children were to have been free according to the old Pennsylvania law. There were two uncles of the family who were also to have been free, but who had been kept over time; so they sued for their freedom, and gained it. The lawyers in the case were abolitionists and friends to the slaves, and saw that these men had justice. After they had secured their freedom, they entered suit for my wife's mother, their sister, and her seven children. But as soon as the brothers entered this suit, Robert Logan, who claimed my wife's mother and her children as his slaves, put them into a trader's yard in Lexington; and, when he saw that there was a possibility of their being successful in securing their freedom, he put

them in jail, to be "sold down the river." This was
a deliberate attempt to keep them from their rights,
for he knew that they were to have been set free,
many years before; and this fact was known to all the
neighborhood. My wife's mother was born free, her
mother, having passed the allotted time under a law,
had been free for many years. Yet they kept her
children as slaves, in plain violation of law as well as
justice. The children of free persons under southern
laws were free — this was always admitted. The
course of Logan in putting the family in jail, for safe
keeping until they could be sent to the southern
market, was a tacit admission that he had no legal
hold upon them. Woods and Collins, a couple of
"nigger traders," were collecting a "drove" of
slaves for Memphis, about this time, and, when they
were ready to start, all the family were sent off with
the gang; and, when they arrived in Memphis, they
were put in the traders' yard of Nathan Bedford
Forrest. This Forrest afterward became a general in
the rebel army, and commanded at the capture of
Fort Pillow; and, in harmony with the debasing
influences of his early business, he was responsible
for the fiendish massacre of negroes after the capture

of the fort — an act which will make his name forever infamous. None of this family were sold to the same person except my wife and one sister. All the rest were sold to different persons. The elder daughter was sold seven times in one day. The reason of this was that the parties that bought her, finding that she was not legally a slave, and that they could get no written guarantee that she was, got rid of her as soon as possible. It seems that those who bought the other members of the family were not so particular, and were willing to run the risk. They knew that such things — such outrages upon law and justice — were common. Among these was my Boss, who bought two of the girls, Matilda and her sister Mary Ellen. Matilda was bought for a cook; her sister was a present to Mrs. Farrington, his wife's sister, to act as her maid and seamstress. Aunt Delia, who had been cook, was given another branch of work to do, and Matilda was installed as cook. I remember well the day she came. The madam greeted her, and said: "Well, what can you do, girl? Have you ever done any cooking? Where are you from?" Matilda was, as I remember her, a sad picture to look at. She had been a slave, it is true, but had seen good days to what the slaves down the river saw. Any one could see she was almost heart-broken — she never seemed happy. Days grew into weeks and weeks into months, but the same routine of work went on.

### MY MARRIAGE — BIRTH OF TWINS.

Matilda had been there three years when I married her. The Boss had always promised that he would give me a nice wedding, and he kept his word. He was very proud, and liked praise. The wedding that he gave us was indeed a pleasant one. All the slaves from their neighbor acquaintances were invited. One thing Boss did was a credit to him, but it was rare among slave-holders — he had me married by their parish minister. It was a beautiful evening, the 30th of November, 1858, when Matilda and I stood in the parlor of the McGee house and were solemnly made man and wife. Old Master Jack came up from Panola at that time, and was there when the ceremony was performed. As he looked through his fingers at us, he was overheard saying: "It will ruin them, givin wedins-wedins." Things went on as usual after this. The madam grew more irritable and exacting, always finding fault with the servants, whipping them, or threatening to do so, upon the slightest provocation, or none at all. There was something in my wife's manner, however, which kept the madam from whipping her — an open or implied threat perhaps that such treatment would not be endured without resistance or protest of some kind. This the madam regarded as a great indignity, and she hated my wife for it, and, at times, was ready to crush her, so great was her anger. In a year there were born to us twin babies; and the madam now thought she had my wife tied, as the babies would be a barrier to anything like resistance on her part, and there would be no danger of her running away. She, therefore, thought that she could enjoy, without hindrance, the privilege of beating the woman of whose womanhood she had theretofore stood somewhat in fear.

MADAM'S CRUELTY TO MY WIFE AND CHILDREN.

Boss said from the first that I should give my wife assistance, as she needed time to care for the babies. Really he was not as bad as the madam at heart, for she tried to see how hard she could be on us. She gave me all the extra work to do that she could think of, apparently to keep me from helping my wife in the kitchen. She had all the cooking to do for three heavy meals each day, all the washing and ironing of the finest clothes, besides caring for the babies between times. In the morning she would nurse the babies, then hurry off to the kitchen to get breakfast while they were left in charge of a little girl. Again at noon she repeated her visit to the babies, after cooking the dinner, then in the evening, after supper, she would go to nurse them again. After supper was over, dishes all washed and kitchen in order, she would then go to the little ones for the night. One can see that she had very little time with the children. My heart was sore and heavy, for my wife was almost run to death with work. The children grew puny and sickly for want of proper care. The doctor said it was because the milk the mother nursed to them was so heated by her constant and excessive labors as to be unwholesome, and she never had time to cool before ministering to them. So the little things, instead of thriving and developing, as was their right, dwindled toward the inevitable end. Oh! we were wretched our hearts ached for a day which we could call our own. My wife was a Christian, and had learned to know the worth of prayer, so would always speak consolingly. "God will help us," she said: "let us try and be patient." Our trial went on, until one morning I heard a great fuss in the house, the madam calling for the yard man to come and tie up my wife, as she could not manage her. My wife had always refused to allow the madam to whip her; but now, as the babies were here, mistress thought she would try it once more. Matilda resisted, and madam called for Boss. In a minute he came, and, grabbing my wife, commenced choking her, saying to her: "What do you mean? Is that the way you talk to ladies?" My wife had only said to her mistress: "You shall not whip me." This made her furious, hence her call for Boss. I was in the dining room, and could hear everything. My blood boiled in my veins to see my wife so abused; yet I dare not open my mouth. After the fuss, my wife went straight to the laundry. I followed her there, and found her bundling up her babies' clothes, which were washed but not ironed. I knew at a glance that she was going away. Boss had just gone to the city; and I did not know what to say, but I told her to do the best she could. Often when company came and I held the horses, or did an errand for them, they would tip me to a quarter or half a dollar. This money I always

saved, and so had a little change, which I now gave
to Matilda, for her use in her effort to get away from
her cruel treatment. She started at once for Forrest's
trader's yards, with the babies in her arms and, after
she got into Memphis, she stopped outside the yard to
rest. While she was sitting on the curb stone, Forrest came out of the yard by the back gate and saw
her. Coming up to her he said: "My God! Matilda,
what are you doing here? You have changed so I
would not have known you. Why have you come
here?" Matilda said: "I came back here to be sold
again." He stepped back and called another "nigger
trader," Collins by name, from Kentucky. "Look
here," said Forrest, pointing to my wife. Collins
took in the situation at once and said he would buy
her and the children. "That woman is of a good
family," said he, "and was only sold to prevent her
from getting her freedom." She was then taken into
the yard. "Oh!" said Forrest, "I know these McGees, they are hard colts." Word was then sent McGee that his cook was in the yard and had come to be
sold. He went in haste to the yard. Collins offered
to buy her, but McGee said no man's money could buy
that woman and her children. I raised her husband

and I would not separate them. She was brought back, and as they rode along in the rockaway, Boss said: "When I am through with you I guess you won't run away again." As they drove up I saw the madam go running out to meet them. She shouted to Matilda: "Ah! madam, you put up at the wrong hotel." They at once went to the barn where my wife was tied to the joist, and Boss and the madam beat her by turns. After they had finished the whipping, Boss said, tauntingly: "Now I am buying you and selling you I want you to know that I never shall sell you while my head and yours is hot." I was trembling from head to foot, for I was powerless to do anything for her. My twin babies lived only six months after that, not having had the care they needed, and which it was impossible for their mother to give them while performing the almost endless labor required of her, under threats of cruel beatings. One day not long after our babies were buried the madam followed my wife to the smoke house and said: "I am tempted to take that knife from you, Matilda, and cut you in two. You and old Ruben (one of the slaves) went all around the neighborhood and told the people that I killed your babies, and almost whipped you to death." Of course, when the slaves were accused falsely, as in this case, they were not allowed to make any reply— they just had to endure in silence whatever was said.

### EFFORTS TO LEARN TO READ AND WRITE.

Thomas, the coachman, and I were fast friends. We used to get together every time we had a chance and talk about freedom. "Oh!" Tom would say, "if I could only write." I remember when Tom first began to take lessons at night from some plasterers, workmen of the neighborhood. They saw that he was so anxious to learn that they promised to teach him every evening if he would slip out to their house. I, too, was eager to learn to read and write, but did not have the opportunity which Tom had of getting out at night. I had to sleep in the house where the folks were, and could not go out without being observed, while Tom had quarters in another part of the establishment, and could slip out unobserved. Tom, however, consoled me by saying that he would teach me as soon as he knew how. So Tom one night put a copy of some figures on the side of the barn for me to practice from. I took the chalk and imitated him as near as I could, but my work was poor beside his, as he had been learning for some months, and could make the figures quite well and write a little. Still I kept trying. Tom encouraging me and telling me that I would learn in time. "Just keep trying," said he. When this first lesson was over, I forgot to rub out the marks on the barn, and the next morning when Old Master Jack, who happened to be at our home just at that time, went out there and saw the copy and my imitation of it, he at once raised great excitement by calling attention to the rude characters and wanting to know who had done that. I was afraid to own that I had done it; but old Master Jack somehow surmised that it was Tom or I, for he said to Boss: "Edmund, you must watch those fellows, Louis and Thomas, if you don't they will get spoilt—spoilt. They are pretty close to town here—here." Tom and I laughed over this a good deal and how easily we slipped out of it, but concluded not to stop trying to learn all we could. Tom always said: "Lou, I am going to be a free man yet, then we will need some education; no, let us never stop trying to learn." Tom was a Virginian, as I was, and was sold from his parents when a mere lad. Boss used to write to his parents (owners) occasionally, that his people might hear from him. The letters were to his mother, but sent in care of the white folks. Tom had progressed very fast in his secret studies, and could write enough to frame a letter. It seems it had been over a year since Boss had written for him, but nothing was said until one morning I heard Boss telling Tom to come to the barn to be whipped. He showed Tom three letters which he had written to his mother, and this so startled him that he said nothing. I listened breathlessly to each word Boss said: "Where did you learn to write?" asked he, "and when did you learn? How long have you been writing to your mother?" At that moment he produced the three letters which Tom had written. Boss, it seems, had mistrusted something, and spoke to the postmaster, telling him to stop any letters which Tom might mail for Virginia to his mother. The postmaster did as directed, for slaves had no rights which postmasters were bound to respect; hence, the letters fell into the master's hands instead of going to their destination. Tom, not hearing from his first letter, wrote a second, then a third, never dreaming that they had been intercepted. Boss raged and Tom was severely whipped. After this nothing Tom did pleased any of the family—it was a continual pick on him. Everything was wrong with both of us, for they were equally hard on me. They mistrusted, I think, that I could write; yet I could not find out just what they did think.

### TOM STRIKES FOR LIBERTY AND GAINS IT.

Tom stayed only a few weeks after this. He said to me, one morning: "Lou, I am going away. If I can get a boat to-night that is starting off, why, I am gone from this place." I was sad to see him go, for he was like a brother to me — he was my companion and friend. He went, and was just in time to catch the boat at the Memphis dock. He succeeded in getting on, and made an application to the captain to work on the boat. The captain did not hesitate to employ him, as it was common for slaves to be permitted to hire themselves out for wages which they were required to return, in whole or in part, to their masters. Of course all such slaves carried a written pass to this effect. Tom was shrewd; and, having learned to write fairly well, he wrote himself a pass, which was of the usual kind, stating his name, to whom he belonged, and that he was privileged to hire himself out wherever he could, coming and going as he pleased. Where the slave was an exceptional one, and where the owner had only two or three slaves, a pass would readily be given to hire himself out, or hire his own time, as it was generally called, he being required to turn over to his master a certain amount of his earnings, each month or week, and to make a report to his master of his whereabouts and receipts. Sometimes the slave would be required to turn in to his master a certain sum, as, for instance, fifty or one hundred dollars a year; and he would have to earn that before he could use any of his earnings for himself. If he was a mechanic he would have little trouble in doing this, as the wages of such were often quite liberal. This kind of a pass was rarely, if ever, given by the planters having large numbers of slaves. Another kind of pass read something like this: "Pass my boy or my girl," as the case might be, the name being attached. These were only given to permit the slave to go from the farm of his own master to that of another. Some men had wives or children belonging on neighboring farms, and would be given passes to visit them. Without such a pass they were liable to be stopped and turned back to their homes. There was, however, a good deal of visiting without passes, but it was against the general rule which required them; and any slave leaving home without a pass was liable to punishment if discovered. On our plantation passes were never given, but the slaves did visit in the neighborhood, notwithstanding, and would sometimes slip into town at night. Tom had in this way seen the pass of a neighboring slave to hire out; and it was from this he learned the form from which he wrote his, and which opened his way to freedom. Upon reading Tom's pass, the captain did not hesitate, but hired him at once; and Tom worked his way to New Orleans, to which city the boat was bound. In the meantime Boss took me and we drove to numerous stations, where he telegraphed ahead for his run-away boy Tom. But Tom reached New Orleans without hindrance, and there fell in with the steward of a Boston steamer, and, getting aboard of it, was soon on the ocean, on his way to that city where were so many friends of the slave. Arriving there he made his way to Canada; which was, for so many generations, the only land of freedom attainable to American slaves.

NEWS OF TOM'S REACHING CANADA.

Now that Tom was gone, excitement prevailed at

the house among the white folks—nothing had been heard of him or the method of his escape. All the servants expected that he would be caught, and I was alarmed every time Boss came from the city, fearing that he had news that Tom was caught. He had been gone about six months, when, one morning, I went to the postoffice and brought back a letter. It seemed to me that I felt that it contained something unusual, but I did not know what it was. It proved to be a letter from Tom to Boss. They did not intend that the servants should know it was from Tom, but one of the house maids heard them reading it, and came out and told us. She whispered: "Tom is free; he has gone to Canada; Boss read it in the letter Lou brought." This news cheered me, and made me eager to get away; but I never heard from him any more until after the rebellion. Tom gone made my duties more. I now had to drive the carriage, but Uncle Madison was kept at the barn to do the work there, and hitch up the team. I only had to drive when the family went out.

### M'GEE EXPECTS TO CAPTURE TOM.

In the summer the McGees made up their minds to go down east, and come around by Niagara Falls, for this was the place from which Tom had written them. Boss had great confidence in himself, and did not doubt his ability to take Tom home with him if he should meet him, even though it should be in Canada. So he took a pair of handcuffs with him as a preparation for the enterprise. His young nephew had been to Niagara Falls, and seen and talked with Tom; but Boss said if he had seen him anywhere he would have laid hands on him, at once, and taken him home, at all hazards.

### MAKING CLOTHES.

When the family went on this visit down east I was left in charge of the house, and was expected to keep everything in order, and also to make the winter clothes for the farm hands. The madam and I had cut out these clothes before she left, and it was my principal duty to run the sewing machine in their manufacture. Many whole days I spent in this work. My wife made the button holes and sewed on the buttons. I made hundreds of sacks for use in picking cotton. This work was always done in summer. When the garments were all finished they were shipped to the farm at Bolivar, to be ready for the fall and winter wear. In like manner the clothes for summer use were made in winter.

### A SUPERSTITION.

It was the custom in those days for slaves to carry voo-doo bags. It was handed down from generation to generation; and, though it was one of the superstitions of a barbarous ancestry, it was still very generally and tenaciously held to by all classes. I carried a little bag, which I got from an old slave who claimed that it had power to prevent any one who carried it from being whipped. It was made of leather, and contained roots, nuts, pins and some other things. The claim that it would prevent the folks from whipping me so much, I found, was not sustained by my experience—my whippings came just the same. Many of the servants were thorough believers in it, though, and carried these bags all the time.

### MEMPHIS AND ITS COMMERCIAL IMPORTANCE.

The city of Memphis, from its high bluff on the Mississippi, overlooks the surrounding country for a long distance. The muddy waters of the river, when at a low stage, lap the ever crumbling banks that yearly change, yielding to new deflections of the current. For hundreds of miles below there is a highly interesting and rarely broken series of forests, cane brakes and sand bars, covered with masses of willows

and poplars which, in the spring, when the floods come down, are overflowed for many miles back. It was found necessary to run embankments practically parallel with the current, in order to confine the waters of the river in its channel. Memphis was and is the most important city of Tenessee, indeed, the most important between St. Louis and New Orleans, particularly from the commercial point of view. Cotton was the principal product of the territory tributary to it. The street running along the bluff was called Front Row, and was filled with stores and business houses. This street was the principal cotton market, and here the article which, in those days, was personified as the commercial "king," was bought and sold, and whence it was shipped, or stored, awaiting an advancing price. The completion of the Memphis and Charleston railroad was a great event in the history of the city. It was termed the marriage of the Mississippi and the Atlantic, and was celebrated with a great popular demonstration, people coming from the surrounding country for many miles. Water was brought from the Atlantic ocean and poured into the river; and water taken from the river and poured into the Atlantic at Charleston. It was anticipated that this railroad connection between the two cities would make of Charleston the great shipping port, and of Memphis the principal cotton market of the southwest. The expectation in neither of these cases has been fully realized. Boss, in common with planters and business men throughout that whole region, was greatly excited. I attended him and thus had the opportunity of witnessing this notable celebration.

## CHAPTER III.

## SLAVERY AND THE WAR OF THE REBELLION.

### BEGINNING OF THE WAR.

I remember well when Abraham Lincoln was elected. Boss and the madam had been reading the papers, when he broke out with the exclamation: "The very idea of electing an old rail splitter to the presidency of the United States! Well he'll never take his seat." When Lincoln was inaugurated, Boss, old Master Jack and a great company of men met at our house to discuss the matter, and they were wild with excitement. Was not this excitement an admission that their confidence in their ability to whip the Yankees, five or six to one, was not so strong as they pretended?

The war had been talked of for some time, but at last it came. When the rebels fired upon Fort Sumpter, then great excitement arose. The next day when I drove Boss to town, he went into the store of one Williams, a merchant, and when he came out, he stepped to the carriage, and said: "What do you think? Old Abraham Lincoln has called for four hundred thousand men to come to Washington immediately. Well, let them come; we will make a breakfast of them. I can whip a half dozen Yankees with my pocket knife." This was the chief topic everywhere. Soon after this Boss bought himself a six shooter. I had to mould the bullets for him, and every afternoon he would go out to practice. By his direction, I fixed a large piece of white paper on the back fence, and in the center of it put a large black dot. At this mark he would fire away, expecting to hit it; but he did not succeed well. He would sometimes miss the fence entirely, the ball going out into the woods beyond. Each time he would shoot I would have to run down to the fence to see how near he came to the mark. When he came very near to it- within an inch or so, he would say laughingly: "Ah! I would have got him that time." (Meaning a Yankee soldier.) There was something very ludicrous in this pistol practice of a man who boasted that he could whip half a dozen Yankees with a jackknife. Every day for a month this business, so tiresome to me, went on. Boss was very brave until it came time for him to go to war, when his courage oozed out, and he sent a substitute; he remaining at home as a "home guard." One day when I came back with the papers from the city, the house was soon ringing with cries of victory. Boss said: "Why, that was a great battle at Bull Run. If our men had only known, at first, what they afterwards found out, they would have wiped all the Yankees out, and succeeded in taking Washington."

PETTY DISRESPECT TO THE EMBLEM OF THE UNION.

Right after the bombardment of Fort Sumpter, they brought to Memphis the Union flag that floated over the fort. There was a great jubilee in celebration of this. Portions of the flag, no larger than a half dollar in paper money, were given out to the wealthy people, and these evidences of their treason were long preserved as precious treasures. Boss had one of these pieces which he kept a long time; but, as the rebel cause waned these reminders of its beginning were less and less seen, and if any of them are now in existence, it is not likely that their possessors will take any pride in exposing them to view.

As the war continued we would, now and then, hear of some slave of our neighborhood running away to the Yankees. It was common when the message of a Union victory came to see the slaves whispering to each other: "We will be free." I tried to catch everything I could about the war, I was so eager for the success of the Union cause. These things went on until

### THE BATTLE OF SHILOH, APRIL 9, 1862.

Boss came hurrying in one morning, right after breakfast, calling to me: "Lou, Lou, come; we have a great victory! I want to go up and carry the boys something to eat. I want you and Matilda to get something ready as quickly as you can." A barrel of flour was rolled into the kitchen, and my wife and I "pitched in" to work. Biscuit, bread, hoe-cake, ham, tongue—all kinds of meat and bread were rapidly cooked; and, though the task was a heavy one for my wife and me, we worked steadily; and, about five o'clock in the afternoon the things were ready. One of the large baskets used to hold cotton was packed full of these provisions. Our limbs ached from the strain of the work, for we had little help. One reason for the anxiety of the Boss for the preparation of this provision for the soldiers was that he knew so many in one of the companies, which was known as the

"Como Avengers," and he had a son, a nephew and a brother of his wife connected with it; the latter a major on Gen. Martin's staff. On the following morning I got up early, and hurried with my work to get through, as I had to go to the postoffice. Madam hurried me off, as she expected a letter from her husband, who had promised to write, at the earliest moment, of their friends and relatives. I rushed into the city, at full speed, got some letters and a morning paper, and, returning as rapidly as possible, gave them to her. She grasped them eagerly, and commenced reading the paper. In a short time I heard her calling me to come to her. I went in, and she said, in great excitement: "Louis, we want to have you drive us into town, to see the Yankee prisoners, who are coming through, at noon, from Shiloh." I went and told Madison to hitch up, as soon as he could. In the meantime I got myself ready, and it was not long before we were off for the city. The madam was accompanied by a friend of hers, a Mrs. Oliver. We were at the station in plenty of time. About twelve o'clock the train from Shiloh drew into the station; but the prisoners that were reported to be on board were missing—it proved to be a false report. While they were looking for the prisoners, Mrs. Oliver saw Jack, a servant of Edward McGee, brother of madam. "Oh! Look," said Mrs. Oliver, "there is Edward's Jack. Lou, run and call him." In a minute I was off the carriage, leaving the reins in madam's hands. Jack came up to the carriage, and the women began to question him: "Where is your Master, Ed," asked both of them. "He is in the car, Missis--he is shot in the ankle," said Jack. In a minute the women were crying. "I was going to get a hack," said Jack, " to—" "No, No!" said both of them. "Go, Lou, and help Jack to bring him to our carriage. You can drive him more steadily than the hackman." Jack and I went to the car, and helped him out, and after some effort, got him into our carriage. Then I went and got a livery hack to take the women and his baggage home. When we reached home, we found there old Mrs. Jack McGee, mother of the madam, Mrs. Charles Dandridge, Mrs. Farrington, sisters of madam, and Fanny, a colored woman, Edward's housekeeper and mistress—a wife in all but name. All of these had come to hear the news of the great battle, for all had near relatives in it. Mrs. Jack McGee and Mrs. Dr.

Charles Dandridge had each a son in the terrible conflict.

### MOURNING IN MASTER'S FAMILY.

In the afternoon, when all were seated in the library reading, and I was in the dining room, finishing up my work, I happened to look out of the window, and saw a messenger coming up the graveled walk. I went out to meet him. "Telegram for Mrs. McGee," he said. I took it to her; and, reading it without a word, she passed it to the next member of the family, and so it was passed around until all had read it except Mrs. Dandridge. When it was handed to her, I saw, at a glance, that it contained for her the most sorrowful tidings. As she read she became livid, and when she had finished she covered her face with her handkerchief, giving a great, heavy sob. By this time the whole family was crying and screaming: "Oh! our Mack is killed." "Mars, Mack is killed," was echoed by the servants, in tones of heart-felt sorrow, for he was an exceptional young man. Every one loved him—both whites and blacks. The affection of the slaves for him bordered on reverence, and this was true not alone of his father's slaves, but of all those who knew him. This telegram was from Boss, and announced that he would be home the next day with the remains. Mrs. Farrington at once wrote to old Master Jack and to Dr. Dandridge, telling them of Mack's death and to come at once. After I mailed those letters nothing unusual happened during the afternoon, and the house was wrapped in silence and gloom. On the following morning I went for the mail as usual, but there was nothing new. At noon, the remains of the much loved young man arrived at our station, accompanied by Boss and Dr. Henry Dandridge, brother of the father of the deceased, who was a surgeon in the rebel army. I went to the station with another servant, to assist in bringing the body to the house. We carried it into the back parlor, and, after all had been made ready, we proceeded to wash and dress it. He had lain on the battlefield two days before he was found, and his face was black as a piece of coal; but Dr. Henry Dandridge, with his ready tact, suggested the idea of painting it. I was there to assist in whatever way they needed me. After the body was all dressed, and the face painted, cheeks tinted with a rosy hue, to appear as he always did in life, the look was natural and handsome. We were all the afternoon employed in this sad work, and it was not until late in the evening that his father and mother came down to view the body for the first time. I remember, as they came down the broad stairs together, the sorrow-stricken yet calm look of those two people. Mrs. Dandridge was very calm — her grief was too great for her to scream as the others did when they went in. She stood and looked at her Mack; then turning to Boss, she said: "Cousin Eddie, how brave he was! He died for his country." Poor, sorrowing, misguided woman! It was not for his country he died, but for the perpetuation of the cruel, the infamous system of human slavery. All the servants were allowed to come in and view the body. Many sad tears were shed by them. Some of the older slaves clasped their hands, as if in mute prayer, and exclaimed, as they passed by the coffin: "He was a lovin boy." It seems that all his company but five or six were killed. At an early hour next morning the funeral party started for the home in Panola, where the body of the lamented young man, sacrificed to an unholy cause, was buried, at the close of the same day.

Edward stayed at our house some six weeks, his ankle was so slow in getting well. At the end of that time, he could walk with the aid of crutches, and he took Fanny and went home.

### ALARM OF THE MEMPHIS REBELS.

Not long after this the people were very much worked up over the military situation. The Yankees had taken Nashville, and had begun to bombard Fort Pillow. The officials of the Memphis and Ohio railroad company became alarmed at the condition of things, fearing for the safety of their stock. The officers, therefore, set about devising some plan by which they might get the cars down on the Memphis and Jackson road, where they imagined their property would be safe from the now terrible Yankees. The railroad officials at once set to work to buy the right of way through Main street, to give them the connection with the southern road named. At first it was refused by the city authorities, but finally the right of way was granted. When, however, the railroad men began to lay the ties and rails, the people grew furious. Some fled at once, for they imagined that this act of the railroad officials indicated that the Yankees must be coming pretty near. Boss became so excited, at this time, that he almost felt like going away too. The family grew more and more uneasy; and it was the continual talk: "We must get away from Memphis. The companies are already moving their rolling stock, fearing the Yankees may come at any time and destroy everything; we must get away," said Boss, speaking to the madam."

### THE FAMILY FLEE FROM MEMPHIS.

Things continued in this way until about June, 1862. The Union troops had taken Fort Pillow. We had heard the firing of cannon, and did not know what it meant. One morning I was in the city after the mail, and I learned that a transient boat had just come down the river, which had lost a part of her wheelhouse. She was fired on from Fort Pillow, sustaining this serious damage from the shot. This increased the excitement among the people; and our folks became alarmed right away, and commenced talking of moving and running the servants away from the Yankees, to a place of safety. McGee was trying for some time to get some one to take the house, that is, to live in and care for it until after the war, while the family were gone. They never thought that slavery would be abolished, and so hoped to come back again. After some search, they found a widow, a Mrs. Hancock. She was to have full charge of the house and continue keeping boarders, as she had been doing in Memphis. The vaunted courage of this man seems to have early disappeared, and his thought was chiefly devoted to getting his family and his slaves into some obscure place, as far away as possible from the Yankees, that were to be so easily whipped. We were about two weeks getting ready to leave, stowing away some of the things they did not want to move. The Boss and his family, my wife and I, and all the house servants were to go to Panola, to his father's. The family went by rail, but I had to drive through in a wagon.

## I AM TAKEN TO BOLIVAR FARM.

Soon after the family all reached Master Jack's, Boss took me to his own farm in Bolivar county. This separated me for a time from my wife, for she remained with the family. I had to look after the house at the farm, attend the dining room, and, between meals, sew every day, making clothes for the hands. I could run on the machine eighteen to twenty pairs of pants a day, but two women made the button holes and did the basting for me, getting the goods all ready for the machine.

CAPTURE OF A UNION TRADING BOAT.

The Yankees had made a raid through Bolivar, before I came, and the excitement had not abated, as they were spreading themselves all through the state. There was a Union trading boat, the Lake City, that had been successful in exchanging her goods for cotton that came from Memphis. She usually stopped at Helena, Fryer's Point and other small towns; but on a trip at this time she came about fifty miles farther down the river, to Carson's Landing, right at Boss' farm. She was loaded with all kinds of merchandise—sugar, tobacco, liquor, etc. She had a crew of about forty men, but they were not well prepared for a vigorous defense. The rebel soldiers stationed in the vicinity saw her as she dropped her anchor near the landing, and they determined to make an effort for her capture. They put out pickets just above our farm, and allowed no one to pass, or stop to communicate with the boat. Every one that sought to pass was held prisoner, and every precaution taken to prevent those on the boat from learning of the purposes of the rebels, knowing that the boat would land in the morning, if not informed of the danger, and then it was anticipated that they could easily make her a prize. There was a small ferry boat behind the steamer, and as the latter dropped down stream, and then steamed up to the landing, the former stood off for a few moments. As the steamer touched shore, the rebels charged on her, and captured her without a struggle. In the meantime the ferry boat, seeing what had happened, sped away up stream, the soldiers firing at her, but doing little damage, except the breaking of the glass in the pilot house. The rebels, seeing that the ferry boat had escaped them, turned their attention to the unloading of the steamer. They sent out for help in this work, and the summons was answered by the neighbors far and near. Wagons were brought, two of which were from our farm, and loaded with goods, which were taken to Deer Creek, forty miles from Carson Landing. What goods they found themselves unable to carry away were packed in the warehouse. The steamer was then burned. McGee was present, and the rebel captain gave him a written statement of the affair to the effect that the residents were not responsible for it, and that this should be a protection for them against the Union forces. The officers and crew of the steamer to the number of forty were made prisoners, and taken to

Deer Creek, the rebel headquarters of that region, and put in the jail there. The ferry boat that escaped went to Helena, Arkansas, and carried the news of the affair to the Union forces there.

### BOSS TAKEN PRISONER.

I was told by Boss to take my stand on our veranda, and keep watch on the river, and if I saw any boat coming down to let him know at once. I kept a close watch the next morning until about eight o'clock, when I saw a boat, but she had almost gone past our house before I discovered her. I ran into the house and told Boss. He ordered me to get his horse at once, which I did; and he mounted and went down to the landing as fast as he could. Upon reaching there, he was taken prisoner by the Union soldiers, who had just landed from the boat. All who came near were captured. The Union soldiers went to work and transferred all the goods which the rebels had put into the warehouse from the boat which they had captured, then setting fire to the warehouse and the postoffice, they pushed off yelling and shouting with glee. Among those captured by the Union soldiers were three other rich planters besides Boss, all of whom were taken to Helena. After they had been there about a week, the planters offered to secure the release of the Unionists captured on the boat which the rebels had burned at Carson Landing, and who had been sent to the rebel jail at Deer Creek, if they were guaranteed their own release in exchange. They offered to bear the expense of a messenger to the rebel officer, at Deer Creek, with this proposition. The Union officer at Helena accepted the proposition, and the messenger was sent off. It was arranged that he should stop over at our house, both on his way down and back. Upon his return, he stopped over night, and the next morning proceeded on his way. When he had gone about five miles, he saw a flat-boat at a landing, on which were people drinking and having a merry time. He stopped, and went aboard; and, in joining the carousal, he soon became so intoxicated that he was unable to go on with his journey. Among those present was one Gilcrease, a cousin of the McGees, who recognized the man as the messenger in this important business, went to him and asked him for the letters he carried. The fellow refusing to give them up, Gilcrease took them from him, and at once sent to our overseer for a reliable man by whom to forward them to the commandant at Helena. The overseer called me up from the cabin to his room, and told me that I was to go to Helena to carry some important papers, and to come to him for them in the morning, and make an early start. I left him and went back to my cabin.

### MY THIRD EFFORT FOR FREEDOM.

I made up my mind that this would be a good chance for me to run away. I got my clothes, and put them in an old pair of saddle bags — two bags made of leather, connected with a strip of leather, and used when traveling horseback for the same purpose as a satchel is used in traveling in the cars. I took these bags, carried them about a half mile up the road, and hid them in a fence corner, where I could get them in the morning when I had started on my trip. Fryer's Point, the place to which I was to go, was about fifty miles from the farm. I started early in the morning, and, after I had gone twenty-five miles, I came to the farm of William McGee, a brother of the madam, and stopped to change horses. I found that William McGee was going, in the morning, down to old Master Jack's; so I took one of their horses, leaving mine to use in its place, went right to Fryer's Point, delivered the letters to a man there to carry to Helena, and got back to William McGee's farm that night. I made up my mind to go with William down to Panola, where madam was, to tell her about Boss being captured. The next morning, he started, and Gibson, his overseer and myself accompanied him. He questioned me about the capture of Boss, what the soldiers had done, etc., and I told him all I knew of the matter. "Well, Lou," he said, "why did you not bring us some whisky?" "I did bring a little with me," I said. He laughed, saying: "Oh, well, when we come to some clear water we will stop and have a drink." Then I said: "Mr. Smith will look for me to-night, but he wont see me. I am going to tell the madam that Boss is captured." "Hey, ho!" he said, "then you are running away." I replied: "Well I know Miss Sarah dont know Boss is in prison." We traveled on, all three of us, stopping at intervals to be refreshed. After two days, we arrived at Panola. Our journey was a tedious one. The streams were so swollen in places that we could hardly pass. The Tallehatchie we had to swim, and one of the men came near losing his horse and his life. The horses became tangled in a grape vine, as we were nearing the shore at which we aimed, and, the current being very swift, we were carried below the landing place; but, finally, we got safely ashore, McGee landing, and we following. Reaching Panola, wet and weary, I conveyed to madam the story of her husband's capture and imprisonment, a rumor of which had already reached her.

The next morning was Christmas, and a number of the family had come to spend it together. They had heard that McGee was captured and in prison; but, now, as I told them every feature of the affair in detail, they grew excited and talked wildly about it. Among those who came were Dr. Dandridge and his wife, Blanton McGee and his wife, Tim Oliver and his wife. All these women were daughters of old Master Jack McGee, and sisters to the madam. Mrs. Farrington and old lady McGee were already there. These re-unions on Christmas were a long established custom with them, but the pleasure of this one was sadly marred by the vicisitudes and calamities of the war. A shadow hung over all the family group. They asked me many questions about Boss, and, of course, I related all I knew.

After I had been there three days, they started me back with letters for Boss. When I left it was near night, and I was to stop over at Master Jack's farm fifteen miles away. It was expected that I would reach Fryer's Point on the third morning, thus allowing me three days to go sixty miles; but I could not make much headway, as the roads were so heavy. The understanding was that I was to deliver the letters to the same gentleman, at Fryer's, to whom I delivered the others, for forwarding to Boss at Helena. I was then to go straight to the farm at Boliver, and report to Smith, the overseer. But after I had got about four miles away, I concluded that I would not go back to the farm, but try to get to the Yankees. I knew I had disobeyed Smith by going down to the madam's to tell her about Boss, because he told me not to go when I spoke to him about it. And now if I went back I feared he would kill me; for I knew there would be no escape for me from being run into the bull ring, and that torture I could not think of enduring. I, therefore, stopped, and, taking the bridle and saddle from the horse, hid them in the corner of a fence in a cornfield. Then I went into the woods. The papers which I had were in the saddle-bag safe. The place where I stayed in the daytime was in a large shuck-pen — a pen built in the field to feed stock from, in the winter time. This pen was on Dr. Dandridge's farm; and the second night I worked my way up near the house. Knowing all the servants, I was watching a chance to send word to the coachman, Alfred Dandridge, that I wanted him to tell my wife that I was not gone. I went down to his cabin, in the quarters; and, after a short time he came. I was badly scared, and my heart was heavy and sore; but he spoke comfortingly to me, and I was cheered, somewhat, especially when he promised to see Matilda, and tell her of my whereabouts. He gave me some food, and hid me away for the night in his house. I kept close all the next day; and, at night, when all was still, Alfred and I crept out, and went to old Master Jack's. The distance was not great, and we soon covered it. Alfred went in and told my wife that I was outside and wanted to see her. She came out, and was so frightened and nervous that she commenced sobbing and crying, and almost fainted when I told her, in low tones, that I was going to try to get to Memphis, and that Alfred was helping to plan a way to this end. The rebels occupied both roads leading to Memphis, and I was puzzled to know how to reach the city without coming in contact with them. Two days after I had talked with my wife, the rebel troops who were camped on the Holly Springs road left for some other point. My friend Alfred found this out, and came and told me the encouraging news. The following night I went to old Master Jack's and told my wife that the way now seemed clear, and that I was going at once. I was bent on freedom, and would try for it again. I urged my wife not to grieve, and endeavored to encourage her by saying that I would return for her, as soon as possible, should I succeed in getting to a land of freedom. After many tears and blessings, we parted, and I left, Uncle Alfred going with me some three miles, as I was not acquainted with the road. When he left me I went on alone with gloomy forebodings, but resolved to do my best in this hazardous undertaking, whatever might happen. The road passed over hills and through swamps, and I found the traveling very wearisome. I had travelled some hours, and thought I was doing well; when, about one o'clock in the night, I came up out of a long swamp, and, reaching the top of a hill, I stopped for a moment's rest, raising myself to an erect position from that of walking, inclined by reason of weariness and the weight of the saddle-bags thrown across my shoulders. The weather was bad, a heavy mist had come up, and it was so dark that I could hardly see my way. As I started on, a soldier yelled at me from the mist: "Halt! advance and give the countersign." I stopped immediately, almost scared out of my wits. "Come right up here," said the soldier, "or I'll blow you into eternity." I saw at once he was a rebel soldier. I knew not what to do. This place where I was halted was Nelson's farm, and the house was held as headquarters for a company of rebel soldiers, known as bushwhackers. While they belonged to the rebel army, they were, in a measure, independent of its regulations and discipline, kept back in the woods, ready for any depradation upon the property of unionists — any outrage upon their persons. The soldier who had halted me took me up to the house, and all began to question me. I told them that I had been sent on an errand, and that I had lost my way. The next morning I was taken about a mile away down in the swamp, over hills and through winding paths, till at last we came to the regular rebel camp. I was in great fear and thought my end had come. Here they began to question me again — the captain taking the lead; but I still stuck to my story that I had been sent on an errand, and had lost my way. I knew that this was my only chance. They tried to make me say that I had come from the Yankees, as they were in camp near Holly Springs. They thought the Yankees had sent me out as a spy; but I said the same as at first—that I had lost my way. A soldier standing by said: "Oh! we will make you talk better than that;" and stepping back to his horse, he took a sea-grass halter, and said: "I'll hang you." There was a law or regulation of the rebel government directing or authorizing the hanging of any slave caught running away; and this fellow was going to carry it out to the letter. I talked and pleaded for my life. My feelings were indescribable. God only knows what they were. Dr. Carter, one of the soldiers, who knew me and the entire McGee family, spoke up and said: "You had better let me go and tell Mr. Jack McGee about him." The captain agreed to this, and the doctor went. The following day, Old Jack came, and steadily refused to consent to my being hung. He said: "I know Edmund would not have him hung-ung. He is too valuable-aluable. No, no! we will put him in jail and feed him on bread and water—too valuable a nigger to be hung-ung."

They tried again to make me say that I was with the Yankees. They whipped me a while, then questioned me again. The dog-wood switches that they used stung me terribly. They were commonly used in Mississippi for flogging slaves—one of the refinements of the cruelty of the institution of slavery. I refused to say anything different from what I had said; but when they had finished whipping me I was so sore I could hardly move. They made up their minds to put me in jail at Panola, twenty-two miles away, to be fed on bread and water. The next day was Sunday, and all arrangements having been made for taking me to the place appointed for those whose crime was a too great love for personal freedom, they started with me, passing on the way Old Master Jack's, where they halted to let him know that his advice respecting me was to be carried out. The old man called to my wife: "Come out and see Louis." Some one had told her that they were going to hang me; and I shall never forget her looks as she came out in the road to bid me good-by. One of the soldiers was softened by her agony, and whispered to her: "Don't cry, aunty, we are not going to hang him—we will only put him in jail." I saw this

changed my wife's looks in a minute. I said a few
words to her, and, with a prayer for God's blessing on
us both, we parted, and they moved on. After we had
gone about seven miles, we met two soldiers, who belonged to the regiment at Nelson. They said:
"Hello! where you going with that nigger?" The
two men in charge of me replied: "We are going to
take him to Panola jail." "Why," said one of the
soldiers, "there is no jail there; the Yanks passed
through and pulled down the doors and windows of
the jail, and let all the prisoners out." This caused
a stop; and a council of war was held in the fence
corner, the result of which was a decision to take me
back to old Jack McGee's. After we had gotten back
there, they took me and gave me another flogging to
satisfy the madam. I was never so lacerated before.
I could hardly walk, so sore and weak was I. The
law was given me that if ever I was caught out in the
public road again, by any soldier, I was to be shot.
Monday morning I was sent to the field to plow; and,
though I was very stiff and my flesh seemed sore to
the bone, my skin drawn and shriveled as if dead, I
had, at least, to make the attempt to work. To have
said: "Master, I am too sore to work," would only

have gotten me another whipping. So I obeyed without a word.

### REBELS BURN THEIR COTTON.

The capture of Memphis by the Union troops closed the principal cotton market of the country, and there was, as a consequence, an immense accumulation of the product in the hands of the farmers of that region. They were, therefore, compelled to resort to temporary expedients for its protection from the elements. Old Master Jack had his piled up in a long rick, and shelters built over it. Other farmers did the same. As cotton was almost the only source of revenue for the farmers, and as there was now no opportunity of getting it to market, there was such a dearth of money as had seldom, if ever, been known, and a corresponding dearth of those necessaries of life which money was the only means of procuring. The accumulations of our family in this product were very great. While the rebel farmers were waiting for a time when they could turn their stores of this valuable article into money, a proclamation was issued by the rebel government that all the owners of cotton that had it stored on their farms must prepare to have it burned. Hundreds of rebel soldiers marched to every section of Mississippi that they could reach, and applied the torch to these cotton ricks. The destruction was enormous. This was to prevent the cotton from falling into the hands of the Unionists. Jeff Davis said to his deluded followers that it was better for them to destroy this property than to risk its coming into the possession of their enemies, since that would equally impoverish themselves, while it might result to the pecuniary advantage of those with whom they were at war. I know that it was a terrible sight when our cotton was burned. Hundreds of bales were consumed, and it seemed like a wholly unnecessary destruction of property, and, therefore, unwise as a war measure. Many were sorry that they had acquiesced in the policy, as it cost them thousands of dollars, and made many poor. They thought that possibly their farms might have escaped the visits of the Union soldiers, and the property, so much needed, been saved in whole or in part. They reasoned, and reasoned correctly, that their condition would in no sense have been worse if their cotton had not been burned by their own soldiers, but might have been much better in many cases, without any real detriment to the rebel cause. The sacrifice of the property of their own people, by the rebel authorities, was evidence of the desperation of the condition of the rebellion, and was so regarded by not a few at that time. Those were terrible days. One could see anxiety written on every face among the whites. The slaves even looked worried at times, though the war meant so much to them, as they were always looking forward to freedom, at its close, if the Union troops were successful.

### MY FOURTH RUNAWAY TRIP.

After I had been working on the farm about two months, and had thoroughly talked the matter over with Alfred Dandridge, we planned to make a careful and persistent effort to escape from the land of bondage. We thought that as others, here and there, all through the neighborhood, were going, we would make trial of it. My wife and I were at old Master Jacks; and, after we had consulted with Alfred and Lydia, his wife, we all concluded to go at once. Alfred had been a teamster for Dandridge for many years, and was familiar with the road, as he had hauled cotton into Memphis for his master for so long a time he could hardly tell when he began. Matt Dandridge was a fellow servant, belonging to the same man, and both had, as was not unusual, taken their master's name, or, rather, were known by it. Matt had learned of our purpose to run away, and concluded to join our party. So one night, when all was still, we started. Uncle Alfred, as I always called him, was to be our leader. He was older than any of the rest of us, and had had a good deal of experience; we, therefore, all looked to him—in fact, we relied entirely upon him. After we had traveled about twelve miles, we came to a swamp, called Hicke-Halley. Here we stopped, as day was dawning, and settled down for the day, as we could travel only in the night, lest we should be seen and caught. We were wet our clothes soaked through from the heavy dew. We had to travel through corn fields, cotton patches, oat fields and underbrush, not daring to take the main road. This is why we were so wet. Uncle Alfred traveled wholly by the stars—they were his guide. He knew by looking at them the four cardinal points of the compass. Many old slaves were guided in this way when traveling in the night, and some could tell the time of night by the position of the stars. We stayed in Hicke-Halley all day, and in the evening, when it was dark enough, we started on again, Uncle Alfred offering up a prayer to God to guide us safely through. Cold Water was our next stopping place, and here a difficulty rose before us that made us fearful. We had nothing to wear but what we had on, and not much of that, so had small space for carrying anything, and, therefore, had brought with us only a little bite to eat. As we had lived on this small provision for a day, there was now but little left for our increasing wants; and the difficulty of securing anything from the houses without danger of detection was almost insurmountable. But we felt encouraged as we thought of what we were striving for, and sped on our way. But the way was hard, for sometimes we got completely stuck in brier patches, and had to turn and go back, in order to find a way out. Old logs and driftwood, that had been piled up year after year, were other obstacles in our way; and one can imagine how hard it was to make our way through such a mass of brush and forrest by the dim light of the stars as they struggled through the dense branches of the trees. We stumbled on, however, as best we could, each fearful, yet silently praying for guidance and help. When within four or five miles of Cold Water, Uncle Alfred stopped, and cautioned us not to speak above a whisper, as the rebel troops were camped on both sides of us. We were in a swamp between the two roads, gradually working our way through to the river, as we could not go on either of the roads for fear of detection. At the bridges, where these roads crossed the river, there were rebel camps, and it was useless for us to think of crossing either. We, therefore, worked our way carefully through the thicket that we were in until we came within sight of the river. Then Uncle Alfred went ahead, creeping a few steps, then stopping to see if the river was clear of soldiers. From this point it was some two and a half miles to the bridges, each way; and it was our idea that if we could cross here without being seen by the soldiers, we would be all right. Uncle Alfred came back to us and told us that he thought the way was clear. "I can not hear a sound," said he, "so let us go on." We followed the river down until we came to a place where we could cross. Here we found some drift-wood—an old tree had been blown down, nearly across the river, leaving a space of about twenty feet. Over this natural bridge we crept to the open space which we waded, the water being up to our knees; but we did not mind this. There was no talking above a whisper, for fear of being heard by the soldiers. Daylight had begun to dawn, and we felt good that we had succeeded thus far. We went on quietly until we got entirely out of the swamp and reached some hills. The woods were on each side of us and still thick; so we stopped here, on the side of a hill, where the sun shone brightly on us, expecting to rest for the day. Our clothes had already become quite dry from the sunshine; and, so far, we felt all right. Alfred and I had made a turn around the place, listening to see if we could hear any noise, or see any trace of soldiers; but we discovered no trace of them, and went back to our stopping place. I had been asleep and some of the others were still asleep, when suddenly I heard the yelp of blood hounds in the distance. It seemed quite far away at first, but the sound came nearer and nearer, and then we heard men yelling. We knew now that they were on our trail, and became so frightened that we all leaped to our feet, and were about to run, when Uncle Alfred said: "Stop children, let me oil you feet." He had with him a bottle of ointment made of turpentine and onions, a preparation used to throw hounds off a trail. All stopped;

and the women, having their feet anointed first, started off, Uncle Alfred telling them to run in different directions. He and I were the last to start. Alfred said: "Don't let the bushes touch you;" at the same time he ran through the bushes with such a rattling noise one could have heard him a great distance. He wore one of those old fashioned oil cloth coats made in Virginia; and, as he ran, the bushes, striking against the coat, made a noise like the beating of a tin board with sticks. The funny part of it was that, having cautioned us to be careful about noise, he made more than all of us. By this time the woods were resounding with the yelping of the hounds and the cries of their masters. The hounds numbered some fourteen. The men howled and cheered in concert with the brutes, for they knew that they were on the right trail, and it would be but a short time before they caught us all. I had gotten further away than any of them. Having run about a mile, I came to a farm, and started across an open field, hoping to reach a wood beyond, where I might conceal myself. Before I was half way across the field, on looking back, I saw the dogs coming over the fence, and knowing there was no chance of my getting to the woods, I turned around, and ran back to a persimmon tree, and just had time to run up one of the branches when the dogs came upon the ground. I looked and saw the men, Williams the nigger-catcher, and Dr. Henry and Charles Dandridge. As soon as Williams rode up, he told me to come down, but I was so frightened I began to cry, yet came down trembling. The dogs laid hold of me at once, tearing my clothes and biting my flesh. Dr. Dandridge was just riding up, and seeing what was happening, yelled out to Williams: "I thought your dogs didn't bite." "Oh! well," said Williams, "he aint hurt—we've got to let 'em bite a little."

They took us all back to the fence where I crossed over, all the others having been caught. Our hearts were filled with dismay. All looked as if they were condemned to be hung. We knew not what was to be done with us. The women were pitiful to see, crying and moaning—all courage utterly gone. They started back with us to Old Master Jack's, at Panola, and we stopped for the night at a small farm house. The old woman who kept it said, tauntingly: "You niggers going to the Yankees? You all ought to be killed." We started on the following morning, and got back home at one o'clock in the afternoon. All of us were whipped. All the members of the family were very angry. Old Lady Jack McGee was so enraged that she said to my wife: "I thought you were a Christian. You'll never see your God." She seemed to think that because Matilda had sought freedom she had committed a great sin.

### INCIDENTS.

Ever since the beginning of the war, and the slaves had heard that possibly they might some time be free, they seemed unspeakably happy. They were afraid to let the masters know that they ever thought of such a thing, and they never dreamed of speaking about it except among themselves. They were a happy race, poor souls! notwithstanding their down-trodden condition. They would laugh and chat about freedom in their cabins; and many a little rhyme about it originated among them, and was softly sung over their work. I remember a song that Aunt Kitty, the cook at Master Jack's, used to sing. It ran something like this:

> There'll be no more talk about Monday, by and by,
> But every day will be Sunday, by and by.

The old woman was singing, or rather humming,

it one day, and old lady McGee heard her. She was busy getting her dinner, and I suppose never realized she was singing such an incendiary piece, when old Mrs. McGee broke in upon her: "Don't think you are going to be free; you darkies were made by God and ordained to wait upon us." Those passages of Scripture which refer to master and servants were always cited to us when we heard the Word preached; and they were interpeted as meaning that the relation of master and slave was right and proper— that they were rightly the masters and we the slaves.

I remember, not long after Jeff Davis had been elected president of the Confederacy, that I happened to hear old Master Jack talking to some of the members of the family about the war, etc. All at once the old man broke out: "And what do you think! that rascal, Abraham Lincoln, has called for 300,000 more men. What is Jeff Davis doin'-doin'?" He talked on, and seemed so angry that he gave no one a chance to answer: "Jeff Davis is a grand rascal-rascal," said he, "he ought to go into the field himself." At first all the Southerners were jubilant over Davis; but as they were losing so, and the Unionists gaining, they grew angry and denounced him oftentimes in unsparing terms.

## UNION RAID AT MASTER'S FARM.

During the time the Union headquarters were at Helena, a Union gun-boat came down the river as far as Boliva, and stopped at Miles McGee's. The soldiers made a raid through the farm, taking chickens, turkeys, meat and everything that they could lay hands on. During this raid Miles McGee came out of the house with a gun, and shot the commanding officer of the party. He became alarmed over what he had done, and hid in the cabin of one of the servants. He never came near the house. The Union soldiers came three different times to catch him, but never succeeded. The last time they came, he made for the canebrake, and hid himself there until they were gone. But though he had escaped their righteous vengeance, he became so nervous that he left his hiding place in the canebraker, and went to Atlanta, Ga., and staid there among friends until things became more quiet. At last wearying of this, he determined to return to old Master Jack's, but not to his own home. Word had been received of his coming, and great preparations were made for his reception. After he had started on his return, he was taken ill on the train, and was left at a small town called Jackson, where he soon died.

I drove the family to the depot upon the day of his expected arrival, and as the train came in, the women waved their handkerchiefs; and, when the conductor stepped off, they asked him if Mr. McGee was aboard. He said no—"I have his remains." The scene that followed, I can not describe—such wailing and screaming! I could not but feel sad, even though they had treated me so meanly, causing the death of my children, and separating me from my wife. Their grief was indeed great. The sad news was conveyed to his mother, old Mrs. Jack McGee, at the house by an advance messenger, and we soon followed with the body. He was the favorite son of his mother, and her grief was very great. But for his wanton shooting of the Union officer, he would probably not have met his death as he did.

### UNION SOLDIERS PASS THE PANOLA HOME.

One winter night, while I was at old Master Jack's, I was awakened by a rumbling noise like that of heavy wagons, which continued steadily and so long a time that I finally concluded it must be an army passing, and such I found to be the case, upon getting up and venturing out, the rumbling which had awakened me being caused by the passing artillery.

I was afraid to go out straight to the soldiers, but would take a few steps at a time, then stop and listen behind a tree or the shrubbery. All seemed quiet—there was no talking. I had listened about twenty minutes when there seemed to be a halt at the creek, some distance from the house. Soon afterwards I heard the command given: "Forward!" I at once made up my mind that they were Yankee soldiers. I got on my knees and crawled to the fence, not daring to go openly, fearing that they might hear or see me and shoot, supposing me to be a spy. I went back into the house and told my wife that they were Yankees who had just passed. "Uncle George," said I. "this would be a good time for us to go." "Oh, no," said he, "we are not quite ready." Uncle George's cabin was where my wife and I stayed while at old Master Jack's. In the morning I was to carry a parcel to Como, a place not far from home, to Mr. James McGee, who was in the rebel army. It was not quite daylight when I made ready to go on my trip, for I was anxious to find out more about the soldiers. Going to the stable and saddling my horse, I mounted and rode out to the big gate leading to the main road, just as day was dawning. As I dismounted to open the gate, some soldiers were passing and an officer sung out to me, "Hello! which way are you going." I said "to Como, to carry this parcel of clothing to my young master in the war." "You have a fine horse," said the officer, "I guess I will exchange horses with you." He took my package of clothing and some letters which I had to mail and my horse, leaving me his, which was a very poor animal. I was badly scared at this peformance, fearing that I would be severely whipped for the loss of the horse and package. Yet how could I help it? We knew nothing but to serve a white man, no matter what he asked or commanded. As a matter of course, I did not go to Como, as I had nothing to take—the officer had everything, but went back to the cabin. I supposed that the soldiers had all passed; but in about half an hour Aunt Kitty, on looking out of her cabin window, exclaimed: "My God! just look at the soldiers!" The yard was covered with the blue coats. Another venerable slave said: "My Lord! de year of jubilee am come." During the excitement I ran to the big house, and told the madam that the Yankees were there, and had taken my horse and every thing I had. Old Master Jack had heard the news, but was not able to come out. He had arisen, but, when he knew of the presence of the Yankees, he went back to bed, calling for Kitty to get him a mush poultice. "Tell Kitty-ity-ity to get me a mush poultice-oltice." It was customary, after the beginning of the war, for him to take sick, and call for a poultice to be put upon his stomach whenever he heard of the Yankees being near. He and many like him were especially valorous only when the blue coats were far away. The soldiers went into the dairy and drank all the milk, helped themselves to butter, cheese, meat, bread and everything in sight which they wanted. Nothing was said to them by the white folks, but the slaves were glad, and whispered to each other: "Ah! we's goin' to be free." Old Master Jack, lying on his couch would ask every little while: "Where are they? Are they gone?" After they had all left the premises, he said: "My God! I can't stand it. Them devils-evils are just goin' through the country destroyin' everything." I was sent down to get Uncle Peter for old master, and when Peter came up the old man asked: "Well, did any of the servants go away? And, sir, them devils took Louis' horse and the clothes he had for his young master."

## HIDING VALUABLES FROM THE YANKEES.

Right after this the McGees commenced planning to put away their valuables, to keep them from the Union soldiers. All the servants had to fill up their bed-ticks with fine gin cotton—the lint part—for safe keeping. Great boxes and barrels were packed full of their best things, and put into the cellar, under the house. It was not exactly a cellar, but a large shallow excavation, which held a great deal. We put all the solid silver ware, such as cake baskets, trays, spoons, forks, dishes, etc., in boxes, and buried them under the hen house. Great packages of the finest clothing I had to make up, and these were given in charge of certain servants whose duty it was to run into the big house and get them, whenever they heard that the Yankees were coming, and take them to their cabins. This was a shrewd arrangement, for the soldiers never went into the cabins to get anything. When the soldiers had passed, these packages were taken back to the house. It speaks well for the honesty and faithfulness of the slaves that such trusts could be devolved upon them, notwithstanding all the cruelties inflicted upon them by their masters.

#### DEATH TO RUNAWAY SLAVES.

It was about this time, that the law or regulation of the rebel government was promulgated, authorizing or directing the shooting or hanging of any slave caught trying to get away to the Union army. This barbarous law was carried out in many cases, for every little while we would hear of some slave who was caught running away, and hung or shot. A slave belonging to Boss, ran away, and got safely within the Union lines; but he returned to get his sister. They both got away from the house, but had gone only a few miles, when William McGee overtook them, and shot the man dead. William boasted of this, but told Uncle Peter, the foreman, that he never wanted it mentioned.

#### SLAVES HUNG AND LEFT TO ROT AS A WARNING.

Two slaves belonging to one Wallace, one of our nearest neighbors, had tried to escape to the Union soldiers, but were caught, brought back and hung. All of our servants were called up, told every detail of the runaway and capture of the poor creatures and their shocking murder, and then compelled to go and see them where they hung. I never shall forget the horror of the scene—it was sickening. The bodies hung at the roadside, where the execution took place, until the blue flies literally swarmed around them, and the stench was fearful. This barbarous spectacle was for the purpose of showing the passing slaves what would be the fate of those caught in the attempt to escape, and to secure the circulation of the details of the awful affair among them, throughout all the neighborhood. It is difficult at this day for those not familiar with the atrocities of the institution of slavery to believe that such scenes could ever have been witnessed in this or any other civilized land, as a result simply of a human being's effort to reach a portion of the country, where the freedom of which it was said to be the home, could be enjoyed without molestation. Yet such was the horrible truth in not one case alone, but in many, as I know only too well.

RUNAWAY SLAVE CAUGHT AND WHIPPED.

One day while I was waiting at dinner, some of the children from the slave quarters came running into the house, and said to old Master Jack: "Uncle John is going away—he is down to the creek." He had been put in the carpenter shop, fastened in the stocks, but by some means he had gotten the stocks off his feet, and got lose. All in the house immediately got up and ran out. Old master told me to run and catch the runaway. I did not like to do it, but had to obey. Old master and I ran in pursuit, and soon overtook him. He could not run, as the stocks were still on his arms and neck. We brought him back, and he was "staked out"—that is, four stakes were driven into the ground, the arms tied to two and the legs to the other two. He was then paddled with the whipping paddle upon the bottom of his feet, by old Master Jack, until blood blisters arose, when he took his knife and opened them. I was then sent for salt and water, and the bruises of the suffering chattel were washed as usual in the stinging brine.

A HOME GUARD ACCIDENTALLY SHOOTS HIMSELF.

After the capture of Memphis by the Union forces, the soldiers were in the habit of making raids into the surrounding country. These were a source of alarm and anxiety among the people, and they were constantly on the watch to defend their property and themselves, as best they could. One day Dr. Charles Dandridge went over to one of our neighbors, Mr. Bobor's, to practice shooting, and to see if he had heard anything new about the war. It was the custom of the home-guards to meet weekly, and practice with their fire-arms, in order to be the better prepared, as they pretended, for any sudden incursion of the now dreaded Yankee. Mr. Bobor had gotten a Yankee pistol from some friend, who was in the army, and Dr. Charles wanted to see and try it. It was shown him, and its workings explained. He took it and began shooting, and in showing the other men how quickly he could shoot a Yankee, and mount his horse, he accidentally shot himself under the short rib near his heart, and fell to the ground. All the men came running to him, picked him up and carried him into the house, immediately sending word to Mrs. Dandridge and Master Jack McGee, his father-in-law. The boys came hurrying in, and told us what had happened. I hitched up and drove Boss over to Mr. Bobor's. We found the wounded man rapidly sinking; and when, a little later, his wife came, he could not speak—only clasped her hand. He died that night, and we carried his body to the home, which so short a time before, he had left in health and high spirits.

No casket was to be had—everything of that kind had been consumed or shut out by the war. Accordingly two slaves were ordered to make a coffin, which they did, using plain boards. It was then covered with black alapaca from a dress of the madam, and lined with the cloth from Mrs. Dandridge's opera cloak. The regular material used for these purposes was not to be had. By the time the coffin was ready, the body was so bloated, that it could not be got into it. Resort was then had to a plain box, and in this the body of another of the stricken family group was laid away. At the suggestion of old Master Jack, the coffin was put up in the carriage house, for safe keeping, he saying it would do for him to be burried in. Sorrow had come to this family with such crushing force, that their former pride and boastful spirit had given place to utter dejection.

### SUBSTITUTES FOR COFFEE.

During the war everything was scarce and dear, and substitutes were devised for many of those things which had formely been regarded as the necessaries of life. Sweet potatoes were peeled, then cut in small pieces and put out in the sun to dry. They were then used as a substitute for coffee, when that article became so scarce, toward the close of the war. Great quantities of this preparation were used. Okra was another substitute for coffee. It was dried in the pod, then the seeds shelled out, and these were dried again and prepared something as the coffee is. This made a delicious drink when served with cream, being very rich and pleasant to the taste. Quinine was a medicine that had been of almost universal use in the south; yet it became so scarce that it was sold at seven dollars a bottle, and could not often be had at that price. Lemon leaves were used as a substitute in cases of chills and fever. The leaves were made into a tea, and given to the patient hot, to produce prespiration. During an attack of chills, I was treated in this manner to some advantage. At any rate I got well, which can not always be said of all methods of treatment.

## CHAPTER IV.

## REBELLION WEAKENING—SLAVES' HOPES STRENGTHENING.

M'GEES SLAVES TAKEN TO ALABAMA.

While I was absent on my last runaway trip, the Yankees had made a raid through Panola; and our people had become greatly frightened. As soon as they had got back with me and my fellow runaways, they assembled a gang of slaves for the purpose of taking them to Atlanta, Ga., to get them out of the reach of the Union soldiers. Among the slaves selected for the transfer were myself, my wife Matilda, and the seamstress. The others all belonged to Dr. Dandridge and Blanton McGee. Both the Drs. Dandridge went with us to Atlanta. We traveled across the country until we came to Demopolis, Alabama, where we found Boss camped on the bank of the Tombigbee river with all the farm slaves from Bolivar county. This was the first time I had seen Boss since he was captured and taken to Helena. As my wife and I were the only ones in the gang who belonged to Boss, we left those with whom we had come and joined his gang. We all then went aboard a boat and were taken to the salt works, situated on the Tombigbee, ninety miles from Mobile. These salt works belonged to the rebel government. The first president of the works was Mr. Woolsey, of Salem, Alabama. During Mr. Woolsey's term, the first part of 1864, when we had been there some time, he wrote to Boss asking if he would sell myself and wife, and offering $3,000 for both of us. Boss was indignant at this and curtly refused. My wife acted as cook at the salt works, in the headquarters for the president, managers and clerks. Mr. Woolsey was delighted with her cooking; her bread and rolls, he said, could not be surpassed.

### M'GEE'S GREAT SCHEME.

When the election of officers of the works came off in the fall, Mr. Gallatin McGee was chosen president. Boss then hired us all, about 100 in number, to labor in these works, but he, of course, received all the revenue. The work assigned me was that of butler at headquarters, and my wife was cook. Both women and children, as well as men, were employed in these works. After some months labor here, soon after Gallatin McGee became president, Matilda and I were removed to the Montgomery headquarters, where we remained until nearly Christmas. A few days before that time, Boss came to Montgomery and arranged for us to meet him in Mobile. We started at the appointed time, reached the city in the morning, and I went directly to the hotel where he told me he would be. I found him at once, and he informed me all about his plans for the future, and what he expected to accomplish. He had purchased an island in the bay, a little way from Mobile, where he had decided to establish salt works of his own. All the brick and lumber for the buildings had been carried there, and work upon them was to be commenced immediately after Christmas. He intended to make a home for the family on the island; and, as soon as he could complete the works, to remove all his hands from the government works to his own. He was very enthusiastic over this scheme, claiming that he would make far more money by it than he was then receiving from hiring out his slaves. He told me that he would remain in Mobile two or three days and would go to Panola to spend the holidays, after which he intended to bring all the family to Mobile, and remain there until the island was in readiness to be occupied. There was to be a general break up of the old home, and the beginning of a new manner of life. I stayed in his room at the hotel all the forenoon, listening to his plans; then I went back where my wife was stopping. As I left his room, he said: "Lou," as he always called me, "I will see you and Matilda at the boat this evening." We went to the boat at the appointed time and saw the Boss, but he did not come near us. As the boat was about to put off, I looked and saw him walking up and down the levee, apparently much excited, running his hands nervously through his hair—a habit common to him when he was worried. He seemed greatly distressed. The military situation troubled him, for the Union army had conquered nearly everything; and the fact now stared him in the face that he would soon lose his slaves. He never dreamed in the beginning of the war that the Unionists would conquer, and that the slaves would be freed; but now he saw that not only all his wealth in the bodies and souls of men was slipping away from him, but that much, if not all of the gain which these chattels had brought him was likely to "take wings and fly away."

## M'GEE'S DEATH.

We returned to the salt works the morning after leaving Mobile. Boss remained two days in Mobile, and then started for Panola, the home of his father-in-law; but, on his way, he was taken sick, having contracted a heavy cold which ran into pneumonia, and he lasted only a short time, dying on New Year's day. He had taken cold in bringing the slaves from Bolivar over the river on barges. The river was overflowed about fifty miles out, and the only way he could get the slaves across was by using large barges made of logs. They were several days floating down in this way, before he could get out to the railroad at Jackson, Miss., where he transferred them to the cars. This was too much of an exposure and it killed him.

After Boss died all the plans were changed. Col. Hunting, son-in-law of old Master Jack, came down to the salt works and hired us all out there for another year. This was the beginning of the year 1865. Of master's plans concerning the island and his proposed salt works the family knew little, for they questioned me closely as to what he told me of the matter. What he spent on the island in lumber, brick, etc., was lost, as they knew nothing of the particulars of the

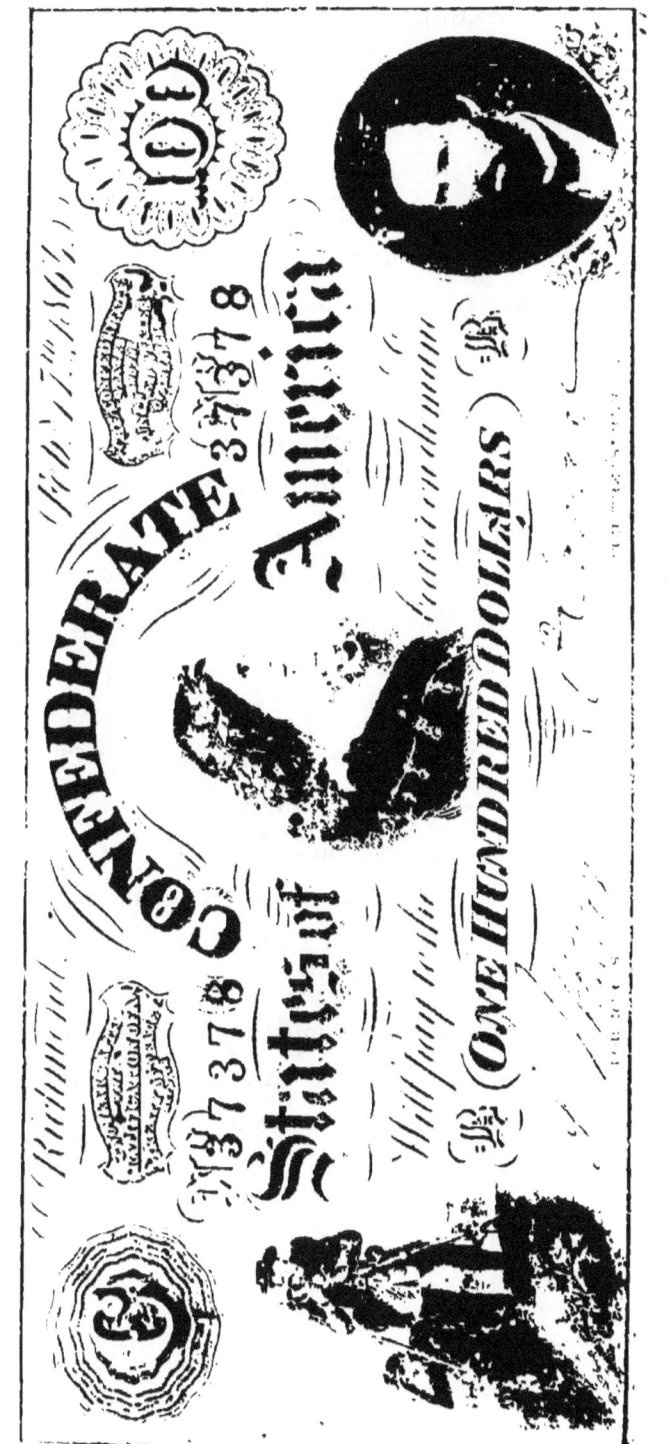

expenditure. The madam remained at her fathers, and the slaves at the works.

### I MAKE SOME MONEY.

As I was here for another year, acting as butler, thought I would try and see if I could not make some money for myself. I asked Mr. Brooks, the manager of the works, if he could get me some tobacco by sending to Mobile for it. He said he could; and on the fourth day thereafter, in the evening, it came. I was anxious to get it the same evening, but Mr. Brooks said: "Oh! I guess you had better wait until morning, then when you finish your work come down to the office and get it—you will then have more time to see the boys in the works." In the morning I was up early, and after doing my morning work I was off to Brooks' office. When I went in he said: "There it is under the table." The package was so small I felt disappointed—a hundred dollars worth ought to be more, said I to myself; but I took it, and went out among the men. I thought I would try to sell it at five dollars a plug, and if I could not sell it at that I would take four dollars. I must make something, for I had borrowed the money to buy it with; and I saw that to clear anything on it, I must at least get four dollars a plug. The money which I had borrowed was from three fellow servants, who had been fortunate in earning some little time and had saved their money. The first man I met in the works bought two plugs, at five dollars each; and after I had been there about an hour all was sold. So I went back with a light heart. Mr. Brooks said to me at dinner: "Well, how did you get along with your tobacco?" "I did very well," I said, "the only trouble was I did not have enough. I sold it for $180." "Well," said he, "if you did, you made more clear money than the works here. How much a plug did you sell it for?" at the same time drawing out his pencil and commencing to figure it up. "I had thirty-six plugs," said I, "and I sold them for five dollars a plug." Nothing more was said just then, but after dinner Brooks and two of the clerks went out on the veranda to smoke. When they were in a good way smoking, Brooks slipped into the dining room, and said: "Well, that was fine; you got five dollars a plug for the tobacco?" "Oh, yes!" I said, "tobacco is scarce, and they were hungry for it; it went like hot cakes—the price was not questioned, I sold at once." "What is the prospect for selling more?" he asked. "Will you sell it

for half the profit if I furnish the tobacco?" I said
"yes." So he sent the same day for a box of tobacco
—about five hundred plugs. When the tobacco came
the box was sawed in two and one-half sent up to my
room. I put some fellows out as agents to sell for me
—Uncle Hudson, who took care of the horses and
mules at the works; John at the hospital; William,
head chopper, among the 100 men in the woods. Each
brought in from $40.00 to $50.00 every two or three
days, and took another supply. Sometimes, when I
had finished my work in the afternoon, I would get an
old pony and go around through the neighborhood
and sell four or five plugs. It was a mystery to the
servants how I got the tobacco; but I did not let on
that Brooks was backing me. In two weeks we had
taken in $1,600.00, and I was happy as I could be.
Brooks was a fine fellow—a northerner by birth, and
did just what he said he would. I received one-half
of the money. Of course this was all rebel money,
but I was sharp, and bought up all the silver I could
find. Just as we got on the other half of the box,
Brooks received word that the Yankees were coming,
and to send all the hands to their masters. I was
glad that I had made some money, knowing that I

would need it if I gained my freedom, which I now knew was quite probable, as the Union forces were gaining ground everywhere. But the message ended my money-making, and I prepared to go home to Panola.

### GOING BACK TO PANOLA.

Mr. Brooks fixed the return papers so that my wife and I could leave the party of slaves at Demopolis, and go on thence to Panola by rail, to convey the news to madam that all hands were coming home; that the Yankees were expected to capture the salt works within a short time. At Jackson, some seven miles from the salt works, we were delayed over night by reason of lack of facilities for crossing the Tombigbee river. The report that the Yankees were coming through had created a panic among the white people; and hundreds, fleeing from their homes, had gathered at the river, waiting and clamoring for an opportunity to cross. Though slaves were property, and valuable on that account, the whites seemed to think that their own lives were in danger, and to be protected first. They therefore took precedence of us. In the morning about seven o'clock a steamer was seen coming at a distance; but it could not be dis-

covered at once just what the character of it was.
The whites became alarmed. Some said: "The
Yankees are coming." Other said: "It is a gun
boat they will surely fire on us." But as the boat
drew near the people saw that there was nothing to
fear—it was only the regular passenger boat. Besides
the hundreds of people, there were scores of wagons,
filled with household goods to go over, and the passage was slow and tedious. We finally got across
and traveled as far as Demopolis, where Matilda and
I left the other slaves, and took a train and went on
to Panola. I delivered the papers to the madam from
Brooks, which told her all the particulars concerning
the break up at the salt works. She sent wagons
right away after the other slaves who were coming
back on foot. They were not brought back to Panola;
but were hired out to different farmers along the road
home—some in Jackson, some in Granda and others in
Panola town. These were all small towns in Mississippi. My wife and I went to work at old Master
Jack's, I on the farm and my wife at her old duties in
the house. We longed for freedom, but were content
for the time with hoping and praying for the coming
of the day when it should be realized. It was sad to

see the changes that had come to the white folks. Sorrow had left its impress upon all and we felt it, notwithstanding all that we had suffered at their hands. Boss had willed the homestead in Memphis to Mrs Farrington, and she was getting ready to take possession. He had borrowed a great amount of money from her when he bought the island at Mobile; and the rapid coming on of the end of the rebellion destroyed all prospect of the success of his salt works scheme, even before his death, and really rendered him bankrupt. Hence the transfer of the Memphis property to her was the only way he could make good what he owed her. The madam now had no home, but was compelled to stay with her father, old Master Jack. She was sadly changed—did not appear like the same person. Her troubles and sorrows had crushed her former cruel and haughty spirit. Her mother had died a few months before, and then her husband had followed, dying suddenly and away from home. Then much of her property had been lost, and social pleasures and distinction were gone forever. Who shall say that the wrongs done her poor, helpless slaves were not avenged in this life? The last I knew of her she was still at her father's.

### INCIDENTS.

A servant who belonged to Dr. Dandridge ran away and got to Memphis just affer it was captured by the Union soldiers. He was put into the army and was stationed at one of the entrances to the city. He was to halt all persons passing to or from the city, no difference who they were, and learn their names and their business. Young William McGee and his sister, Miss Cherry, one day went up to Memphis and, to their surprise, were halted by this former servant of their uncle. When they came home they were speaking of it to their father, and old Master Jack said: "And you halted, did you?" "Why, yes," replied William, "we had to do it." "Well," said the old man, "I would have died-died before I would have done it. To think that a servant should have halted you, and one who has belonged to the family like Anderson!" This old man, notwithstanding all his boasting in the absence of immediate danger, was the verriest coward when danger was present; and if he had been in the place of young William, he would have halted with the greatest alacrity.

While at the salt works I had a little experience at nursing. A fellow slave was taken ill, and I was called on to care for him at night. I always liked this work; it was a pleasure to me to be in the sick room. Typhoid fever was a new case to me, but I remembered what instructions Boss had given me about it. I "pitched in" to do what I could; but the fever was so great he lasted only a few days.

### MY FIFTH STRIKE FOR FREEDOM IS A SUCCESS.

We had remained at old Jack's until June, 1865, and had tried to be content. The Union soldiers were still raiding all through that section. Every day some town would be taken, and the slaves would secretly rejoice. After we came back from Alabama we were held with a tighter rein than ever. We were not allowed to go outside of the premises. George Washington, a fellow servant, and Kitty, his wife, and I had talked considerably about the Yankees, and how we might get away. We knew it was our right to be free, for the proclamation had long been issued—yet they still held us. I did not talk much to my wife about going away, as she was always so afraid I would be killed, and did not want me to try any more to escape. But George, his wife and I continued to discuss the matter, whenever we had a chance. We knew that Memphis was headquarters for the Union troops, but how to reach it was the great question.

It was Sunday, and I had driven one portion of the family to church, and George the other. The family was now very large, as the madam and her family were there, in addition to Old Master Jack's, and all could not go in one carriage. On the way back, young William McGee came up through the farm, on horseback, a nearer way home from church, and encountered several servants belonging to some of the neighbors. He asked them what they were doing there, and if they had passes. To this last question all answered no. "Well," said he, "never come here again without having passes, all of you." At this they all quickly disappeared. When Old Jack came home, Will told him what had passed; and he immediately called for George and Uncle Peter, the foreman, and told them that no one not belonging there was to come into the quarters without a pass; and any servant with a pass should be brought to the house, that the pass might be inspected. They thought, or feared, that if the servants were permitted to come together freely they might plan ways of escape, and communicate to each other what they knew about the war and the Yankees. George came out, and finding me, told me what they had said. "No slave from outside is to be allowed on the place," said he. I replied: "If we listen to them we shall be here until Christmas comes again." "What do you mean?" asked George. "I mean that now, today, is the time to make a start." So, late in the afternoon, during the servants' prayer meeting, of which I have heretofore spoken, we thought would be a good time to get away, as no one would be likely to see us. We talked with John Smith, another servant, and told him all about our plan, asking him not to say a word about our being gone until he was through feeding the stock. This would give us another hour to advance on our journey, as the feeding usually took about that time—from six o'clock until seven. Our fear was that we might be overtaken by the bloodhounds; and, therefore, we wished to get as far away as possible before the white people knew we were gone. It was Sunday afternoon, June 26th, 1865, when George and I, having made ready for the start for the Union lines, went to bid our wives good-bye. I told my wife to cheer up, as I was coming again to get her. I said to Kitty, George's wife: "We are going, but look for us again. It will not be with us as with so many others, who have gone away, leaving their families and never returning for them. We will be here again." She looked up at me, smiling, and with a look of resolution, said: "I'll be ready." She was of a firm, daring nature—I did not fear to tell her all my plans. As my wife was so timid, I said as little as possible to her. George and I hurriedly said our farewells to our wives. The parting was heartrending, for we knew the dangers were great, and the chances were almost even that we should not meet again. I could hardly leave my wife, her agitation and grief were so great. But we were off in a few moments. We crept through the orchard, passing through farm after farm until we struck the railroad, about seven miles from home. We followed this road until we reached Senatobia, about half past seven in the evening. We felt good, and, stopping all night, we started the next morning for Hernando, Miss., another small town, and reached there at two o'clock in the afternoon. The most of the bridges had been burned, by the troops, and there were no regular railroad trains. Fortunately, however, flat cars, drawn by horses were run over the road; and on a train of this kind we took passage. On several occasions, the passengers had to get out, and push the car over a bridge, as it was not made so horses could cross on it, the horses meantime being driven or led through the stream, and then hitched to the car again. After we had gone through this process repeatedly, we at last reached Memphis, arriving about seven o'clock Monday evening. The city was filled with slaves, from all over the south, who cheered and gave us a welcome. I could scarcely recognize Memphis, things were so changed. We met numbers of our fellow servants who had run away before us, when the war began. Tuesday and Wednesday we spent in making inquiries; and I visited our old home at McGee's station. But how different it was from what it had been when the McGees were there. All was changed. Thursday we went to see Col. Walker, a Union officer, who looked after the colored folks, and saw that they had their rights. When we reached his office we found it so filled with people, waiting to see him, that we were delayed about two hours, before we had an opportunity of speaking with him. When our turn came, we went in, and told him that we were citizens of Memphis until the fall of Fort Pillow and Donelson, when our master had run us off, with a hundred other slaves, into Mississippi, and thence to the salt works in Alabama. He questioned us as to where we lived in Memphis. I answered: "What is now headquarters of the Union forces was the home of master, Mr. Edmund McGee, who is now dead." After a few minutes, I said: "Colonel, we want protection to go back to Mississippi after our wives, who are still held as slaves." He replied: " You are both free men to go and come as you please." "Why," said I, "Colonel, if we go back to Mississippi they will shoot the gizzards out of us." "Well," said he, "I can not grant your request. I would be overrun with similar applications; but I will tell you what you can do. There are hundreds of just such men as you want, who would be glad of such a scout." We thanked him and left.

### GOING BACK FOR OUR WIVES.

After carefully considering the matter, we concluded to go back to Senatobia and see the captain of the Union troops there. The next day, Friday, we hired a two horse wagon, and made preparations to start on our perilous undertaking Saturday morning. It was our hope to find some one at Senatobia to go with us to Panola, and protect us in the effort to bring away our wives. So, early in the morning, we set out. Our first stop was at Big Springs camping ground, where we made preparations for refreshing ourselves and spending the night. Just as we had finished building a fire, for cooking and keeping off the mosquitoes, two soldiers came riding up to the spring. "Hello," said one, "which way are you traveling?" "We are just from Memphis," said George. "Have you any whisky?" asked one of them. We replied "yes." Will you give a fellow a horn?" We answered the question by handing them the bottle. While they were drinking, George and I stepped aside, and, after a few moments talk, we decided to put the question to them of going with us to get our wives. I asked: "Where are you from?" "Senatobia," replied one. We at once laid our cause before them, telling them what Col. Walker had said regarding our getting some one to go with us on our enterprise. They listened attentively, and when we had finished, one of them asked: "How much whisky have you?" George answered: "Two bottles." "What do you intend to do when you see the captain at Senatobia?" "Lay our complaint before him," said I. "Now my friend," said one of the soldiers, "I am afraid if you go to the captain you will be defeated. But I'll tell you what I'll do. Give my comrade and me one of your bottles of whisky, and we will put you on a straight track. The reason why I say this is that our captain has been sweetened by the rebel farmers. He is invited out to tea by them every evening. I know he will put you off. But I will write a note to some comrades of mine who, I know, will bring you out safe." We agreed at once to this proposition, and gave them the whisky. He wrote the note, and gave it to us, telling us to go to the last tent on the line in the camp, where we would find two boys to whom we should give it. "They are brave," said he, "and the only two I know of that can help you. If they are not there don't give the note to any one else, but wait till they come back, on Tuesday night. I feel satisfied that they will go and help you out." With these words, they rode off. George and I felt good over our prospects.

### A HAZARDOUS TRIP.

The next morning was Sunday, and we started on, reaching Senatobia about eleven o'clock. We went into the camp, following the directions given us, to go to the last tent in the line; but, when we reached there, the soldiers were out. We lingered around the grounds a short time, then went back, and found them there. We gave them the note; and, after reading it, they simply asked us where we had stopped our wagon. I told them outside the village. "Go there," said one of them, "and remain until we come out to see you." Shortly they came out; and, after we had told them what we wanted, the distance to McGee's, which was about nineteen miles from Senatobia, and had given them such other information as they desired, they concluded that they would go. "We want to be back," said I, "before daylight Monday morning, because we must not be seen on the road; for we are well known in that section, and, if discovered, would be captured and killed." "Well," said one of the soldiers, "we will have to go back to camp, and arrange to be excused from roll call this evening, before we can make the trip." They went back to camp; and, in about ten minutes they came out again saying: "All is right; we will go." We gave them each ten dollars; and promised, if they brought us out safely, to give each ten dollars more. It was now about half-past eleven o'clock. They had to go to camp, and slip their horses out cautiously, so as not to be seen by the captain. In half an hour we were on our way; and, after we had ridden some two miles, we were overtaken by the two soldiers. It was Sunday afternoon; and our having a wagon attracted much attention from the farmers as we passed along. They looked at us so sharply that George and I felt decidedly uneasy; yet we kept up courage and pressed steadily on. After a long and weary ride we reached old Master Jack's a little after sundown. The soldiers rode into the yard ahead of us, and the first person they met was a servant (Frank) at the woodpile. They said to him: "Go in and tell your master, Mr. McGee, to come out, we want to see him," at the same time asking for Louis' and George's wives. Young William McGee came out and the soldiers said to him: "We want feed for seventy-five head of horses." McGee said: "We have not got it." Just then George and I were coming up. We drove in at the gate, through the grove, and passed the woodpile where McGee and the soldiers were talking. McGee had just replied: "We have not got that much feed to spare—we are almost out." "Well," said the soldiers, "we must have it," and they followed on right after the wagons. As we drove past them, young McGee went running into the house, saying to his mother: "It is Louis and George, and I'll kill one of them to-night." This raised quite an alarm, and the members of the family told him not to do that, as it would ruin them. As soon as George and I drove up to the first cabin, which was my wife's and Kitty's, we ran in. Kitty met us at the door and said: "I am all ready." She was looking for us. We commenced loading our wagon with our few things. Meanwhile the soldiers had ridden around a few rods and came upon old Master Jack and the minister of the parish, who were watching as guards to keep the slaves from running away to the Yankees. Just think of the outrage upon those poor creatures in forcibly retaining them in slavery long after the proclamation making them free had gone into effect beyond all question! As the soldiers rode up to the two men they said: "Hello! what are you doing here? Why have you not told these two men, Louis and George, that they are free men—that they can go and come as they like?" By this time all the family were aroused, and great excitement prevailed. The soldier's presence drew all the servants near. George and I hurried to fill up our wagon, telling our wives to get in, as there was no time to lose—we must go at once. In twenty minutes we were all loaded. My wife, Aunt Kitty and nine other servants followed the wagon. I waited for a few moments for Mary Ellen, sister of my wife; and as she came running out of the white folks' house, she said to her mistress, Mrs. Farrington: "Good-bye; I wish you good luck." "I wish you all the bad luck." said she in a rage. But Mary did not stop to notice her mistress further; and, joining me, we were soon on the road following the wagon.

### TWO BRAVE MEN.

Those soldiers were brave indeed. Think of the courage and daring involved in this scheme—only two soldiers going into a country of which they knew nothing except that every white man living in it was their enemy. The demand which they made for food for seventy-five horses was a clever ruse, invented by them to alarm the McGees, and make them think that there was a troop of horses near by, and that it would not be safe for them to offer any resistance to our going away with our wives. Had they thought that there were but two soldiers, it is certain that they would have endeavored to prevent us getting away again, and one or more of us would undoubtedly have been killed.

As already stated, nine other slaves followed our wagon, as it moved off. They had no hats on; some were bare-footed,—they had not stopped to get anything; but, as soon as they saw a chance to get away, they went just as they were at the moment. Aunt Kitty was brave and forethoughtful, for during the week we were gone she had baked and cooked a large amount of substantial food that would keep us from starving while on our journey.

At the first road crossing, the two soldiers thought they saw a large troop of soldiers in the distance, and they galloped ahead of us at full speed; but, on arriving at the spot, they found that what they had thought soldiers were only a herd of cattle. They rode on to the next crossing, we following as we conveniently could. Each poor slave was busy with his thoughts and his prayers. Now and then one would hear a moan or a word from some of the party. All were scared, even though the soldiers were with us. We came to the next cross road, and passed that safely. Our fear was that the McGees might get the neighborhood to join them and pursue us, or send the home guards after us; but Providence was seemingly smiling upon us at last, for no one followed or molested us. We moved on all night, until we came to a creek, at four o'clock in the morning of Monday. The banks of the creek were very steep, and as the horses and wagon went down into the stream, the mattress on top of the wagon, upon which my wife and her sister's children were sitting, was thrown off into the water. Immediately the horses stopped, and became balky. It was such a warm night that they did not want to move on out of the water, and would not start, either, until they got ready. As soon as the soldiers saw the mattress slide off with my wife and the children, one of them plunged into the water with his horse, and, in a minute, brought them all out. All had a good ducking — indeed it seemed like a baptism by immersion. The drenched ones were wrapped in old blankets; and, after an hour's delay, we were again on our way. The soldiers said: "Now we must leave you; the time is coming when we must be in camp for roll call. If you are not at our camp when roll call is over, we will come back and see about you." We gave them each the second ten dollars, as agreed upon, and just as they rode to the top of the hill they left us. We had a clear sweep from this point, and we came into Senatobia about nine o'clock in the forenoon. Our two soldier friends, who had brought us out so safely, came out of camp to see us. They cheered us, and seemed glad that they had rendered us service. We stopped at the camp until we had dried our clothes and had some breakfast; and, then, we made our way to Memphis.

### OUT OF BONDAGE AT LAST.

My wife and her sister were shoeless, and the latter had no hat on—she had hurried out of the house in such excitement that she thought of nothing but getting away. Having to walk some of the way, as all could not ride in the wagon at the same time, we were all tired, dirty and rest-broken, and, on the whole, a pitiful crowd to look at, as we came into the city. One venerable old man, bent with age, whose ebony face shone with delight, came running out into the road as we appeared, exclaiming: "Oh! here dey come, God bless 'em! Poor chil'en! they come fannin." We used large palm leaves to fan ourselves with, as we were so warm. Those nine souls that followed us walked the whole distance, arriving shortly after we did. Thousands of others, in search of the freedom of which they had so long dreamed, flocked into the city of refuge, some having walked hundreds of miles.

It was appropriately the 4th of July when we arrived; and, aside from the citizens of Memphis, hundreds of colored refugees thronged the streets. Everywhere you looked you could see soldiers. Such a day I don't believe Memphis will ever see again — when so large and so motley a crowd will come together. Our two soldier rescuers looked us up after we were in Memphis, and seemed truly glad that we had attained our freedom, and that they had been instrumental in it. Only one thing we regret, and that is that we did not learn their names; but we were in so much trouble, and so absorbed in the business which we had in hand—so excited by the perils of our undertaking, that we never thought to ask them their names, or to what regiment they belonged. Then, after we got to Memphis, though we were most grateful for the service which they had rendered us, we were still so excited by our new condition and surroundings that we thought of little else, and forgot that we had no means of establishing, at a later time, the identity of those to whom we owed so much. Freedom, that we had so long looked for, had come at last; and we gave praise to God, blessing the day when we met those two heroes. It is true that we should have been free, sooner or later; still, but for their assistance, my wife and I might never have met again. If I could not have gone back, which I could never have done alone, until long after, such changes might have occured as would have separated us for years, if not forever. Thousands were separated in this manner—men escaping to the Union lines, hoping to make a way to return for their families; but, failing in this, and not daring to return alone, never saw their wives or children more. Thanks to God, we were guided to these brave soldiers, and so escaped from so cruel a fate.

### A WORD FOR MY OLD MASTER.

In closing this account of my years of bondage, it is, perhaps, but justice to say of my old master that he was in some respects kinder and more humane than many other slaveholders. He fed well, and all had enough to wear, such as it was. It is true that the material was coarse, but it was suited to the season, and, therefore, comfortable, which could not truthfully be said of the clothing of the slaves of other planters. Not a few of these did not have sufficient clothes to keep them warm in winter; nor did they have sufficient nourishing and wholesome food. But while my master showed these virtues, similar to those which a provident farmer would show in the care of his dumb brutes, he lacked in that humane feeling which should have kept him from buying and selling human beings and parting kindred—which should have made it impossible for him to have permitted the lashing, beating and lacerating of his slaves, much more the hiring of an irresponsible brute, by the year, to perform this barbarous service for him. The McGees were charitable — as they interpreted the word — were always ready to contribute to educational and missionary funds, while denying, under the severest penalties, all education to those most needing it, and all true missionary effort—the spiritual enlightenment for which they were famishing. Then our masters lacked that fervent charity, the love of Christ in the heart, which if they had possessed they could not have treated us as they did. They would have remembered the golden rule: "Do unto others as ye would that men should do to you." Possessing absolute power over the bodies and souls of their slaves, and grown rich from their unrequited toil, they became possessed by the demon of avarice and pride, and lost sight of the most vital of the Christly qualities.

## CHAPTER V.

## FREEDOM AFTER SLAVERY.

### COMING NORTH.

As before stated, we arrived in Memphis on the Fourth of July, 1865. My first effort as a freeman was to get something to do to sustain myself and wife and a babe of a few months, that was born at the salt works. I succeeded in getting a room for us, and went to work the second day driving a public carriage. I made enough to keep us and pay our room rent. By our economy we managed to get on very well. I worked on, hoping to go further north, feeling somehow that it would be better for us there; when, one day I ran across a man who knew my wife's mother. He said to me: "Why, your wife's mother went back up the river to Cincinnati. I knew her well and the people to whom she belonged." This information made us eager to take steps to find her. My wife was naturally anxious to follow the clue thus obtained, in hopes of finding her mother, whom she had not seen since the separation at Memphis years before. We, therefore, concluded to go as far as Cincinnati, at any rate, and endeavor to get some further information of mother. My wife seemed to gather new strength in learning this news of her mother, meager though it was. After a stay in Memphis of six weeks we went on to Cincinnati, hopeful of meeting some, at least, of the family that, though free, in defiance of justice, had been consigned to cruel and hopeless bondage—bondage in violation of civil as well as moral law. We felt it was almost impossible that we should see any one that we ever knew; but the man had spoken so earnestly and positively regarding my mother-in-law that we were not without hope. On arriving at Cincinnati, our first inquiry was about her, my wife giving her name and description; and, fortunately, we came upon a colored man who said he knew of a woman answering to the name and description which my wife gave of her mother, and he directed us to the house where she was stopping. When we reached the place to which we had been directed, my wife not only found her mother but one of her sisters. The meeting was a joyful one to us all. No mortal who has not experienced it can imagine the feeling of those who meet again after long years of enforced separation and hardship and utter ignorance of one another's condition and place of habitation. I questioned them as to when and where they had met, and how it happened that they were now together. My mother-in-law then began the following narrative:

"When I was sold from the Memphis trader's yard I was bought by a man who lived not far from Memphis. I never heard of any of the children, and knew nothing as to what had become of them. After the capture of Memphis by the Union army, the people to whom I belonged fled from their home, leaving their slaves; and the other slaveholders of the neighborhood did the same. The slaves, left to themselves, at once departed for Memphis, and I among the number. When I had been there but a short time a call was made for nurses to go into the hospital; and, after thinking of it for a few minutes, I concluded to answer the call, and was speedily installed in the work. When I had been there a short time I found, to my great surprise and delight, my eldest daughter was also employed there. She had come to Memphis as I had, because her master's family had fled; and, hearing the call for nurses, had entered the service at once. I can not tell my pleasure in meeting one of my children, for I had never expected to see any of them again. We continued our work in the hospital until Generals Sheridan and Grant said the city was getting too crowded with colored people—there was not room for them; some must be removed. So, large numbers of them were sent to Cincinnati, and my daughter and I were among them. This is why you see us here together."

When she had finished telling this story my wife and I were shedding tears of joy. My sister-in-law, Mary Ellen, whom Boss bought at the same time that he bought my wife, was with us; thus the mother and three daughters had met again most unexpectedly, and in a way almost miraculous. This meeting again of mother and daughters, after years of separation and many vicisitudes, was an occasion of the profoundest joy, although all were almost wholly destitute of the necessaries of life. This first evening we spent together can never be forgotten. I can see the old woman now, with bowed form and gray locks, as she gave thanks in joyful tones yet reverent manner, for such a wonderful blessing.

## IN CANADA.

We did not remain long in Cincinnati, as houses were so scarce we could not get a place to stop in. My wife's mother had but one room, and we could not stay there. We went on to Hamilton, but stayed there only two months. I worked at whatever I could get to do — whitewashing and odd jobs of any kind. The women managed to get washing to do, so that we got on very well. Our aim was when we left Memphis to get to Canada, as we regarded that as the safest place for refugees from slavery. We did not know what might come again for our injury. So, now, as we had found some of my wife's people, we were more eager to go; and, as I could not get any steady work in Hamilton, we made ready to move on. We went straight to Detroit, and crossed over the river to Windsor, Canada, arriving there on Christmas 1865. I succeeded in getting work as a porter at the Iron House, a hotel situated near the landing. Here my wife also was employed, and here we remained until spring; when, as the wages were so small in Windsor, I went over to Detroit to seek for more profitable employment. After some effort, I succeeded in securing a situation, as waiter, in the Biddle House, and remained there two years, when the manager died, and it changed hands; and, much as I disliked to make a change in my work, I found it necessary. An opportunity soon offered of a position as sailor on the steamer Saginaw, which ran from Green Bay to Escanaba, in connection with the railroad.

### A CLEW TO MY BROTHER WILLIAM.

While I was on this boat, one of the men who worked with me said to me, one day: "Have you a brother, Hughes?" I said, "Yes, but I don't know anything about him. We were sold from each other when boys, "Well," said he, "I used to sail with a man whose name was Billy Hughes, and he looked just like you." I told him there were three boys of us; that we were sold to different parties, and that I had never seen either of my brothers since. One brother was named William, but went by the nickname of Billy. "Has this man had his forefinger cut off," asked I. "Oh!" replied he, "I don't know, Hughes, about that." "Well," said I, "this is all I remember about Billy. I accidentally chopped off his forefinger one day, when we were small boys in Virginia. This is the only thing by which I could identify my brother William." Nothing more was said upon the matter, and it dropped out of my mind. I did not realize how important were the words of this man. It never occured to me that he held the clew that might bring us together again.

### WORK IN CHICAGO.

When the sailing season had ended, the steamer tied up at Chicago for the winter. Upon going ashore, I at once tried to get something else to do, for I could not afford to be idle a day. One of the first men I met in Chicago was my old friend and fellow-servant Thomas Bland. He was glad to see me, and told me all about his escape to Canada, and how he had met Will McGee, at Niagara Falls. He was working at the Sherman House, having charge of the coat room. I told him that I had been sailing during the summer, but that the boat was now laid up, and that I was anxious for another job. He said he would try and see what he could do for me. He went to the proprietor of the hotel, Mr. Rice; and, to my surprise and delight, he was so fortunate as to secure me a position as porter and general utility man. My family were still at Windsor, Canada: and, when I had secured this place, I got leave of absence to make them a visit, and went there at once. Two babies had been born only a day before my arrival. I had hoped to be there on the interesting occasion, but was too late. However, I was pleased to find two bright little girls to aid in the family greeting, which was delightful after the months of separation. My wife, her sister Mary and her two children, her mother and the sister we found at Cincinnati were all still here living together.

### ATTENDING NIGHT SCHOOL.

After a visit of two weeks with my family, I returned to Chicago, and began my work at the Sherman House. I was full of energy and hope, and resolved to put forth every effort to make a man of myself, and to earn an honest living. I saw that I needed education, and it was one of the bitterest remembrances of my servitude that I had been cheated out of this inalienable right — this immeasurable blessing. I, therefore, determined to do what was in my power to gain something of that of which I had been cruelly defrauded. Hence I entered the night-school for freedmen, which had been established in the city, and faithfully attended its sessions during the months it was kept open.

## I SETTLE IN MILWAUKEE.

I worked at the Sherman House until August 1868, and, during this time, saw many travelers and business men, and made some lasting friends among them. Among these was Mr. Plankinton. He seemed to take a fancy to me, and offered me a situation in the Plankinton House, soon to be opened in Milwaukee. I readily accepted it for I was not getting a large salary, and the position which he offered promised more. The Plankinton House was opened in September, and I was placed in full charge of the coat room; and, after I had been there some time, I had, in connection with my coat room duties, charge of the bell stand. My wife had charge of the waiter's rooms, a lodging house situated on Second street, one door from Grand Avenue. This was a brick building that stood where the west portion of the Plankinton now stands. The second floor was used as our living rooms; the third and fourth floors constituted the sleeping apartments of the hotel waiters. My wife looked after these apartments, saw that they were clean, and had a general supervision of them.

## BEGIN BUSINESS FOR MYSELF IN A SMALL WAY.

After the hotel had been running a little over a

year, I saw there was a chance for me to make something at laundry work. I was allowed to take washing from any of the guests who desired their work done privately. In this way I worked up quite a business. I still continued my coat room duties, as my wife managed the laundry work. Our laundry business increased so rapidly I deemed it best to change our quarters from Second street to 216 Grand avenue, which seemed better suited for our purpose. Here the business continued to grow until it reached proportions of which we had little idea when we began it.

### MEETING RELATIVES OF MY OLD MASTER.

One day while I was at the Plankinton I happened to be coming through the hall, when whom should I meet but Col. Hunting, son-in-law of old Master Jack McGee, of Mississippi. We came face to face, and I knew him at once, but he only partially recognized me. He said: "I know your face, but can not recall your name." I said: "Don't you know Louis McGee?" He then remembered me at once. "Why," said he, "my wife, my brother and all his family are here. There is a party of us on a pleasure trip through the north." I soon learned that they had visited at Waukesha springs, and had been at the hotel only a few hours, waiting for the boat for Grand Haven. I hastened to bring my wife to see them and got back with her just in time. They were already in the 'bus, but waited for us. We very cordially shook hands with them. They asked me why I had come so far north, and I replied that we kept traveling until we found a place where we could make a good living. They wished us success and the 'bus rolled away.

### FINDING MY BROTHER WILLIAM.

While I was at the Plankinton House many of the traveling men seemingly liked to talk with me when they came to the coat room to check their things. I remember one day when conversing with one of these gentlemen, he asked, all of a sudden: "Say, Hughes, have you a brother?" I answered: "Yes, I had two, but I think they are dead. I was sold from them when a mere lad." "Well," said he, "if you have a brother he is in Cleveland. There is a fellow there who is chief cook at the Forest City Hotel who looks just like you." I grew eager at these words, and put the same question to him that I did to the man on the steamer when I was sailing: "Has he one fore-finger cut off?" He laughed and answered: "Well, I don't know, Hughes, about that; but I do know this: His name is Billy and he resembles you very much. I'll tell you what I'll do, when I go back to Cleveland on my next trip I'll look and see if that fore-finger is off." Now that the second person had called my attention to the fact that there was a man in Cleveland who looked very much like me, I became deeply interested in fact, I was so excited I could hardly do my work. I awaited the agents return with what of patience I could command; and, at last, one day, when I was least expecting him, I was greeted with these words: "Hello, Hughes! I have good news for you." I grew so excited I could hardly stand still. "Well," he said, "you told me that you had a brother whose name was William, but called Billy for short?" "Yes," I said. "Did your brother Billy have his fore-finger chopped off by his brother Louis, when, as boys, they were one day playing together?" "Yes," I replied. "Then I have found your brother," he said. "I have seen the man in Cleveland, and he corroborates your story in every particular. He says that he was born in Virginia, near Charlottesville, and was owned by one John Martin." I knew now, beyond question, that this was my brother William.

Words failed me to express my feelings at this news. The prospect of seeing my brother, lost so many years before, made me almost wild with joy. I thanked the agent for the interest he had taken in me, and for the invaluable and comprehensive information he had brought. He could hardly have done me a greater favor, or bound me to him by a more lasting obligation.

My first step was to arrange for a leave of absence from my work, which I found no difficulty in accomplishing, and by night I was aboard the express going to Cleveland. My excitement did not diminish as I sped on my journey, and the speed of the express was too slow for my eager anticipations. Upon reaching Cleveland I went directly to the hotel where I was told my brother was employed, and inquired at the office for Billy Hughes. A bell boy was summoned to take me around to the department where he was. When we met neither of us spoke for some moments— speech is not for such occasions, but silence rather, and the rush of thoughts. When the first flash of feeling had passed I spoke, calling him by name, and he addressed me as brother. There seemed to be no doubt on either side as to our true relationship, though the features of each had long since faded forever from the memory of the other. He took me to his house; and each of us related his story with such feelings as few can fully appreciate. He told me that he had never heard anything of our mother or brother. He went back to the old home in Virginia, after the close of the rebellion, but could get no trace of her.

As we related our varied experiences—the hardships, the wrongs and sorrows which we endured and at last the coming of brighter days, we were sad, then happy. It seemed, and indeed was, wonderful that we should have met again after so long a separation. The time allotted to my visit with him passed most pleasantly, and all too quickly; and, as I looked into the faces of his wife and children, I seemed to have entered a new and broader life, and one in which the joys of social intercourse had marvelously expanded. When I came to saying good-bye to him, so close did I feel to him, the tie between us seemed never to have been broken. That week, so full of new experiences and emotions can never be erased from my memory. After many promises of the maintenance of the social relations thus renewed, we parted, to take up again the burdens of life, but with new inspiration and deeper feeling.

I came back to my work with renewed vigor, and I could not but rejoice and give praise to God for the blessings that I had experienced in the years since my bondage, and especially for this partial restoration of the broken tie of kindred. I had long since learned to love Christ, and my faith in him was so firmly established that I gave him praise for each and every ray of happiness that came into my life.

### GROWTH OF THE LAUNDRY BUSINESS.

I continued the laundry work, in connection with that at the hotel, until 1874. I had been in the Plankinton House then six years and a half. The laundry business had increased to such an extent that my wife could not manage it all alone. I, therefore, gave up my position at the hotel, and went into the laundry work on a somewhat larger scale than that upon which we had been conducting it. We were still doing business at 216 Grand avenue, and there we remained until 1876; when we removed to more commodious quarters at 713 on the avenue. But we remained there only a few months, when we removed to 134 Fourth street in the rear. The establishment here was fitted up with all modern appliances; but I was not so successful as I anticipated. My losses were heavy; and though the facilities for doing the work were much better than those which we had before possessed, the location was not so accessible or inviting. We, therefore, went back to our former location at 713 on the avenue.

### EMPLOYED AS A NURSE.

Not long after this, Dr. Douglas, a prominent physician of the city at that time, was in failing health, and, wishing a nurse, I was recommended to him for this service by a friend. I served the doctor in this capacity every night for three months. I then went with him to McComb, a village in southern Mississippi, which had been, in the days of slavery, a somewhat famous resort, but which had lost its prestige, and entered upon a general decline; the hotel and all its surroundings presenting the appearance of general dilapidation. I remained here with the doctor for two weeks until they succeeded in getting another person to care for him. I then took a run down to New Orleans.

### A TRIP SOUTH.

On this southern trip I had the opportunity of observing the condition of the country through which we passed. Many of the farms seemed neglected, the houses dilapidated, or abandoned, the fields either uncultivated and overgrown with bushes, or the crops struggling with grass and weeds for the mastery, and presenting but little promise of a paying harvest In some places the bushes and other undergrowth were fifteen feet high, and the landscape was peculiar and by no means inviting. I could remember the appearance of the cotton farms in slavery days; but how changed were things I now saw! They did not look at all like those which I had been accustomed to see. Everything was dismal and uninviting. The entire country passed through in Mississippi looked like a wilderness. This deterioration was the natural result of the devastating war which had swept the country, and to the industrial revolution which followed and to which affairs had not been adjusted.

When I arrived at New Orleans I found the levee filled with fruit. Oranges and bananas were piled in masses like coal, and the scenes in this portion of the city were very different from anything one sees in the north. Among the many places of interest in the city were the cemeteries. Owing to the low level of the ground and its saturation with water, burials are seldom made in graves, but instead in tombs built of brick or marble or other stone, in which are constructed cells running back from the front and of a size and shape sufficient to admit a coffin. Then, as soon as filled, they are sealed up. These tombs contain from two to six or eight, or even more of these cells, and their general appearance from the front is not unlike that of a section of mail boxes in a post office. Other places of interest were the old French market, the public squares and gardens, the old Catholic churches, and some of the relics of slavery days in the shape of pens where slaves were exposed for sale. One of these was in the basement of the Hotel Royal, which would contain several hundred at once, and from which hundreds went to a bondage bitterer than death, and from which death was the only relief.

### I MAKE NURSING MY REGULAR BUSINESS.

I came back to Milwaukee with a new idea. I liked nursing—it was my choice from childhood. Even though I had been deprived of a course of training, I felt that I was not too old to try, at least, to learn the art, or to add to what I already knew. Dr. Douglas gave me a splendid recommendation, and had some cards printed, bearing my name and address.

These I distributed, and thus began the business which I have followed steadily since that time. Dr. Marks very kindly recommended me to well known men needing the service of a nurse, and to his professional associates; and through this means, and through his continued kindness and interest, I have been almost constantly engaged in this work. I am also indebted to Drs. Fox and Spearman and other prominent physicians for recommendations which have resulted in securing me employment which has proved remunerative to me, and which seemed to give entire satisfaction to the sick and their friends. This is no small part of the compensation in the difficult, often wearing, and always delicate duties of the nurse in the sick room. To every true man or woman it is one of the greatest satisfactions to have the consciousness of having been useful to his fellow beings. My duties as nurse have taken me to different parts of the state, to Chicago, to California and to Florida; and I have thus gained no little experience, not only in my business, but in many other directions.

I have endeavored, in the foregoing sketch, to give a clear and correct idea of the institution of human slavery, as I witnessed and experienced it—its brutality, its degrading influence upon both master and slave, and its utter incompatibility with industrial improvement and general educational progress. Nothing has been exagerated or set down in malice, although in the scars which I still bear upon my person, and in the wounds of spirit which will never wholly heal, there might be found a seeming excuse for such a course. Whatever of kindness was shown me during the years of my bondage, I still gratefully remember, whether it came from white master or fellow slave; and for the recognition which has been so generously accorded me since the badge of servitude was removed, I am profoundly and devoutly thankful.

THE END.

www.ingramcontent.com/pod-product-compliance
Lightning Source LLC
Chambersburg PA
CBHW021839230426
43669CB00008B/1015